THE AMERICAN FAMILY

THE AMERICAN FAMILY

Understanding its Changing Dynamics and Place in Society

Edited by

DENNIS G. WISEMAN, PH.D.

*Coastal Carolina University
Conway, South Carolina*

CHARLES C THOMAS • PUBLISHER, LTD.
Springfield • Illinois • U.S.A.

Published and Distributed Throughout the World by

CHARLES C THOMAS • PUBLISHER, LTD.
2600 South First Street
Springfield, Illinois 62704

© 2008 by CHARLES C THOMAS • PUBLISHER, LTD.

ISBN 978-0-398-07835-5 (paper)

Library of Congress Catalog Card Number: 2008028661

Printed in the United States of America
LAH-R-3

Library of Congress Cataloging-in-Publication Data

The American family ; understanding its changing dynamics and place in society / edited by Dennis G. Wiseman.
   p. cm.
 Includes bibliographical references and index.
 ISBN 978-0-398-07835-5 (pbk.)
 1. Family--United States. I. Wiseman, Dennis.
 HQ536.A5477 2008
 306.850973'09045--dc22

2008028661

CONTRIBUTORS

Maria K. Bachman is Professor of English in the Department of English at Coastal Carolina University, and Director of Interdisciplinary Studies & Women's and Gender Studies. She teaches a variety of courses on nineteenth-century British literature and culture, the novel, children's literature, and gender studies. She has edited scholarly editions of Wilkie Collins's *The Woman in White* and *Blind Love*, as well as a collection of critical essays, *Reality's Dark Light: The Sensational Wilkie Collins.* She holds the B.A. in International Affairs from The George Washington University, the M.A. in English from George Mason University, and the Ph.D. in English from the University of Tennessee.

Monair J. Hamilton is Assistant Professor of Health Education in the School of Health, Kinesiology and Sport Studies at Coastal Carolina University. She is a Certified Health Education Specialist (CHES) and her areas of research and expertise include health disparities in minority populations, improving cardiovascular health of youth, and cultural competence for health professionals. Her scholarship activities focus primarily on the issues of health disparities among African-American women and school (K-12) health education. Professor Hamilton earned her Ph.D. in Health Education and Promotion from Kent State University and her Master's of Public Health from Hunter College of the City University of New York.

William E. Hills is Associate Professor of Psychology in the Department of Psychology and Sociology at Coastal Carolina University. His current research interests include the longitudinal effects of violent crime on families in South Carolina and the development of social work as a profession in Russia. His teaching specialties include adult development and gerontology in traditional and online formats and sport psychology. He holds a Ph.D. and M.S. in Psychology from the University of Georgia and a Master's Degree in Social Work from the University of South Carolina.

Julinna C. Oxley is Assistant Professor of Philosophy in the Department of Philosophy and Religion at Coastal Carolina University. Her research focuses on issues in ethics and political philosophy, the family, feminism, ethical issues relating to the family, and the emotions and ethics. Her teaching specializations include feminist philosophy, philosophy of law, ethical theory, and applied ethics. She is co-director of the Jackson Family Center for Ethics and Values' *Summer Ethics Academy* in the College of Humanities and Fine Arts, a program that teaches ethics to sixth graders. She received a Ph.D. from Tulane University, an M.A. from Boston College, and a B.A. from Wheaton College.

Patricia S. Piver is Assistant Professor of Education in the Spadoni College of Education at Coastal Carolina University. Her research includes qualities of middle school teachers and adoption issues in education. Her teaching specialization areas are curriculum and instruction, social studies education, human growth and development, diversity, and educational psychology. She has worked in middle schools and high schools in Georgia and South Carolina and has been a principal for grades K4–12. Professor Piver holds the Ed.D. and M.A. degrees from the University of South Carolina and the B.S. degree from Mercer University. She is the mother of nine adopted children and has nineteen grandchildren.

Nancy C. Ratcliff is Associate Professor of Early Childhood Education in the Spadoni College of Education at Coastal Carolina University. Her journal publications include *Using Authentic Assessment to Document the Emerging Literacy Skills of Young Children; Use the Environment to Promote and Support Learning; The Need for Alternative Techniques for Assessing Young Children's Emerging Literacy Skills; Music, Movement, and More Corn on the Cob;* and *My World of Sound Teacher's Guides.* Her teaching specialization areas are curriculum and instruction, inquiry, and working with families and community. She holds the Ph.D., M.S, and B.S. degrees from Indiana State University.

Nils Ch. Rauhut is Associate Professor in the Department of Philosophy and Religion at Coastal Carolina University. He is author of *Ultimate Questions: Thinking about Philosophy* (2nd Edition) and editor of *Readings on the Ultimate Questions* (2nd Edition). His areas of expertise include ancient philosophy, logic, and German idealism. He received a Ph.D. degree from the University of Washington in Seattle, a M.A. degree from the University of Colorado in Boulder, and an undergraduate degree from the University of Regensburg in Regensburg (Germany).

Michael J. Root received his Ph.D. from the University of New Hampshire. He is Assistant Professor of Psychology in the Department of Psychology and Sociology at Coastal Carolina University where he teaches courses on the history of psychology, cognition, and research methods. His research areas include the history of twentieth century American psychology, deductive reasoning abilities in social exchanges, and effective methods of pedagogy.

Holley E. Tankersley is Assistant Professor of Political Science in the Department of Politics and Geography at Coastal Carolina University where she teaches courses in public policy and American government. Her research is an investigation of the dynamics of policy innovation and diffusion in the context of federalism, and she possesses a particular expertise in social and family policymaking. Her work has appeared in *P.S.: Political Science and Politics* and the *Political Research Quarterly*. A graduate of the MPP program at Georgetown University, she also holds a Ph.D. in political science from the University of Georgia.

Dennis G. Wiseman is Professor of Education in the Spadoni College of Education at Coastal Carolina University. His books include *Effective Teaching: Preparation and Implementation* (3rd Edition), *Best Practice in Motivation and Management in the Classroom* (2nd Edition), *The Middle Level Teachers' Handbook, The Modern Middle School: Addressing Standards and Student Needs,* and *Teaching at the Uni-versity Level: Cross-Cultural Perspectives from the United States and Russia.* His teaching specialization areas are curriculum and instruction, social studies education, and educational psychology. He holds the Ph.D. and M.A. degrees from the University of Illinois at Urbana-Champaign and the B.A. degree from the University of Indianapolis.

Stephanie M. Wright received her Masters and Ph.D. in social psychology from North Carolina State University where her research focused on jurors' attributions regarding mitigating evidence presented in capital trials. She has conducted national and international field research in early childhood scale validation and in provision of services to justice system-involved youth. Her current research interests span the social cognition areas of mental impairment evidence in capital defendants, public attributions regarding terrorist motivations and activities, and the formation of autobiographical memory. She is Assistant Professor of Psychology in the Department of Psychology and Sociology at Coastal Carolina University.

FOREWORD

Many American universities are known for certain identifiable qualities such as the richness of their long histories, the degree programs that they offer, the level of financial support they have received, their athletic programs, and the scholarship of their faculty members. While these special attributes often shape their identities, most American universities also share special societal purposes. For public universities, one shared purpose often is their dedication to and capacity for public service. Public service can be directed to many different aspects of society and come in many different forms. One important audience for such public service is the family.

From the early colonial period in American history, the family has provided stability, protection, nurturing, motivation, and support for young and old. While change in the American family has been significant since colonial times, in terms of definition, make-up, and perhaps even function, the family continues to be that which explains and provides context for human relationships and development. Universities, through their academic programs and the work of their faculties, teach about the family, conduct research on the family, and offer special programs to inform and serve families. It is through this work that universities not only have impact on families that are already formed, but, through their faculties, students, and programs also have impact on families yet to be formed. This impact itself has the potential to sustain, direct, or, in some ways, redirect the further evolution of the family in society. Fields of study such as education, health, political science, philosophy, and psychology and sociology are often seen as natural areas where these relationships are developed. Meaningful exploration, however, is not limited to these disciplines alone.

Particular areas of study present special opportunities for learning not only more about the American family, but about the American society itself. Family-related issues that pertain to the elderly and the family, grandparents as child caregivers, adoption, family policy in political and social arenas, family values and traditions, the family's response and adaptation to societal pressures, the family as teacher, and childrearing practices all represent important areas of investigation. The ongoing debate regarding the mere definition of family, in social, legislative, and political terms, also is of great importance, not only with respect to legal matters, but to matters related to health, the economy, education, and human relationships as well.

Even as the definition of family has changed through the years, from a married man and woman and their children living in the same household to varied definitions today, the family holds a vital place in the fabric of the American society. Whether the family embraces a traditional definition, a single gender parent structure, a structure that doesn't involve marriage of the adult partners, a stepfamily structure, a structure of grandparents as parents, or yet some other structure, the family continues to evolve, remain strong, and be an essential part of the American society.

This book of readings from a group of dedicated faculty at one university makes an important contribution to the study of family. The readings that follow explore the changing dynamics of the American family, the family and family values, the family and its influence on the health of children, adoption and family formation, justice in the family, grandparents and the family, the family's role in the education of young children, psychological perspectives of childrearing in the United States, family policy and the U.S. welfare state, and oral narrative and family roles. These discussions represent valuable ideas and perspectives as contributions to this dynamic field of study. The reader of this text will not only develop a deeper understanding of the American family in the historical sense, but also as it has evolved and continues to evolve in modern times. The cross-disciplinary nature of the text is a strength of this study of the family as it allows for the bringing together of different viewpoints of benefit to professionals, students, and lay-individuals alike. It is through this cross-disciplinary perspective that the American family may be better understood and, in many ways, better appreciated for its historic, present-day, and no doubt future impact on the American society.

David A. DeCenzo
President
Coastal Carolina University

CONTENTS

THE AMERICAN FAMILY

Part I

THE CHANGING AMERICAN FAMILY

The American family has undergone and continues to undergo significant change as the twenty-first century unfolds. To be sure, this change did not begin with the twenty-first century but much, much earlier. Some might posit that change has been ongoing since the very beginning of the idea of family.

On one hand, there remain today many families that represent the traditional definition of family, that being a married man and woman and biological offspring living in the same domicile. In some ways this definition remains very alive and well. On the other hand, additional family definitions are now a part of the mainstream culture being influenced by social changes such as attitudes toward divorce, marriage partners, remarriage, culture, and values along with economic influences and government practices. To be sure, many more families than ever before are comprised of individuals who are not married but cohabiting; these could be individuals of the same or opposite sex. Families today could also be comprised of households of biological children, adopted children, or both, from a single race, multiple races, or mixed races. Too, families could be grandparent headed with one or no biological parents on the scene and where grandparents are engaged in the carrying out of meaningful and important childrearing responsibilities.

Taking these changes further, some families could be dependent largely upon government subsidies to assist in meeting food costs, housing costs, child care costs, etc. Without question, the U.S. government, through certain legislative actions, has played a significant role in the development of the American family and will continue to have

3

an important impact on the evolution of the family in the future. Government programs have influenced the supports that many families enjoy and often times depend on. They also have influenced the actual definition of the family in terms of the relationships between the adults in the household.

While the American family arguably remains strong and vibrant, it has changed and continues to change in ways that would have been unheard of and unrecognizable only a few decades ago. Some of the impetus for this change is economic, but also social, cultural, and governmental. The readings in this section discuss some of the changes in the American family as the family continues to evolve during this century. Included are discussions of the family and its historical evolution, government policy and the family, family values and feminism, grandparenting roles, and adoption.

Chapter 1

THE 21ST CENTURY AMERICAN FAMILY

Dennis G. Wiseman

THE AMERICAN FAMILY – THE PAST AND PRESENT

Perspective on the American family, one might appropriately say the changing American family, differs from individual to individual, perhaps even from context to context. Families are more diverse today than ever before, but, diversity alone does not fully explain the significant and ongoing changing nature of the family. The relationship of marriage to the family; socioeconomic influences; culture; the economy; domestic issues and pressures; divorce; remarriage; single-parent; gay and lesbian families; extended families; and governmental policy all need to be considered in an analysis of today's American family. Skolnick and Skolnick (2007, pp. 1–2) comment:

> Everybody agrees that families have changed dramatically over the past several decades, but there is no consensus on what the changes mean. The majority of women, including mothers of young children, are now working outside the home. Divorce rates have risen sharply. (But they have leveled off since 1979.) Twenty-eight percent of children are living in single parent families. Cohabitation – once called "shacking up" or "living in sin" – is a widespread practice. The sexual double standard – the norm that demanded virginity for the bride, but not the groom – has largely disappeared from mainstream American culture. There are mother-only families, father-only families, grandparents raising grandchildren, and gay and lesbian families. . . .

There is no doubt that the changing family will see more change to come in the future. Still, people appear to be getting as much joy, and sorrow, from the family as they ever have, and seem as dedicated as ever in taking part in family life. While in many parts of the world, the traditional family may seem to be shaken, the institution of family will probably experience a longer life than any nation now in existence. Although any specific family may appear to be fragile or unstable, the family system as a whole is tough and resilient (Goode, 2007, p. 14).

The distinction between those who see marriage as the core of the family and those who embrace greater diversity continues to grow. The definition of marriage itself is witnessing considerable debate. Marriage supporters, traditionalists or conservatives, see childrearing and child-caring as the primary purpose of marriage and oppose changes, primarily societal changes, that are believed to have brought about an increase in divorce, childbearing outside of marriage, couples living together but not in a married relationship and same-sex family arrangements. In support of marriage, Congress passed legislation in 2006 that included $150 million per year for the promotion of marriage (Cherlin, 2008). The logic of the bill was that, by promoting and strengthening marriage, children's well-being, particularly in lower-income families, would be improved (Casper & Bianchi, 2007). Most believe that the legislation was driven, at least in part, by the conservative values brought to the White House by the George W. Bush Administration. Earlier, however, in 1996, under the Bill Clinton Administration, Congress passed the Defense of Marriage Act (DOMA). This legislation identified the government's position toward homosexuality in marriage and stated that the government definition of spouse is a husband or wife of opposite sex from his or her partner.

In support of a broader, more diverse view of family, liberals believe that families of different types should be recognized, whether they include a married couple or not. Many favor extending the legal protection of marriage to same-sex couples, identifying that gay and lesbian couples experience the same kind of intimacy and commitment as opposite-sex couples. Embracing this view, in 2004, Massachusetts became the first state to legalize same-sex marriage. Canada and Spain, in 2005, became the third and fourth countries, following Belgium and the Netherlands, to legalize same-sex marriage.

The definition of family also can change by culture. Western countries such as the countries of Western Europe and the United States, for example, generally reflect a concept of family represented by parents and children where spouses are freely chosen and the marriage is monogamous. In other parts of the world, such as Asia, Africa, and South America, different examples of the family unit may be found, where marriages at times are arranged by relatives and where the family is strongly male-dominated. Beyond a cultural perspective, family also can be viewed from public and private outlooks. The public family is considered as a unit with one adult, or two adults who are related by marriage, partnership, or shared parenthood, taking care of dependents, and the dependents themselves. The private family is seen as two or more individuals who maintain an intimate relationship that they expect will be lasting, or, in the case of a parent and child, until the child reaches adulthood, and who live in the same household (Cherlin, 2008). The public dimension of family addresses the family in terms of the family's contribution(s) to the public welfare and the services that family members provide in taking care of one another, whereas the private dimension encompasses more intimate relationships and emotional support.

Defining the family has been further approached from such aspects as the function of the family, stability and cooperation among family members, and various benefits derived from being in a family. Additionally, feminist theory considers gender roles in family, in particular cultural and social characteristics that separate women and men in a society. While Thorne (1992) identifies that cultural differences are structured in ways that support the power of men over women, it has been suggested that the most comprehensive plan for restoring family to its rightful place in American society comes from feminists who acknowledge the premodern nature of the family, and, at the same time, its interdependence with a fast-changing world economy (Giele, 2007).

Modernity theory, yet another perspective, reflects a view of families as diverse, changing, and developing. Modernity theorists recognize that personal life has changed fundamentally over the last several decades with one result being that individuals are making more and more choices about different aspects of their lives. And, as these choices are made, questions of personal identity are becoming more and more important. The theory contributes to an understanding of family life at a time when individuals must make decisions in uncertain situations for which there are no fixed rules. Virtually all sociologists support the view that most of the differences in the roles and behaviors of men and women are social and cultural in origin. Most Americans take an individualistic view toward family, emphasizing self-reliance, achievement, and cooperation, but also including feelings and emotional satisfaction.

Hernandez (2007) notes that family demographics also have changed dramatically. Significant changes occurred between the mid-1800s and the mid-1900s due to major changes in the fathers' work, the approaching elimination of the nuclear family, and the development of mass education. The period after World War II saw additional changes brought about by the expansion of mothers' participation in the workforce, the increase in one-parent family living arrangements, and the decline and then increase in child poverty. As the baby boom generation moves beyond childbearing age, further changes are anticipated to come through population growth in other countries, coupled with growing U.S. economic opportunities. An increased U.S. population, as a result of immigration and births to present and future immigrants, is anticipated. As of 2000, 20 percent of children in the United States were children of immigrants.

Developing an understanding of the American family today requires a number of areas of investigation such as marriage, divorce, the formation of "new" families, the economy, and the care of children in the home.

Marriage and Divorce

Three different periods of divorce are identified in the United States, beginning with a period of restricted divorce, predominant until the middle of the nineteenth century (Phillips, 1991). The second period ran until 1970; during this period divorce gradually became more accepted and easier to get, in particular for mistreated wives. Marriage in the nineteenth and twentieth centuries saw a gradual change from an economic partnership to an emotional partnership based on love and companionship, with the divorce rate rising substantially in the late 1800s and early 1900s. Over time, divorce changed from something considered as a rare privilege, primarily for wealthy men, to a common, if still not widely accepted act increasingly available to women. The third period of divorce began in 1970 when the state of California became the first state to remove fault as grounds for divorce. This period of virtually unrestricted divorce, popularly referred to as the era of no-fault divorce, has seen divorce available almost without question, except for a waiting period, to any married person who wants one (Cherlin, 2008). With the advent of no-fault divorce, divorce allowed a marriage to be ended as a result of irreconcilable differences (Glendon, 1987), supporting the view that an individual should not have to continue in a marriage that he or she found to be personally unacceptable. Likely at least in part as a result of this change, the divorce rate in the United States presently is the highest in the world, over a third higher than the second and third-ranked nations of New Zealand and Great Britain (Berk, 2005). It has been estimated that between 40 percent and 50 percent of first-time marriages that took place in the 1990s will end in divorce (Amato, 2001).

Study in this area shows that both societal as well as individual factors are associated with divorce. From the societal side, increase in divorce rates are linked to no-fault divorce legislation, cultural changes, and changes in both women's and men's employment opportunities. From the individual side, divorce is linked to low income and employment, age at marriage, race and ethnicity, cohabitation, parental divorce, and spouse's similarity. Some identify that the increase in heterosexual cohabitation, associated with the delay in marriage and increase in divorce, is one of the most significant changes in family life to take place in the latter half of the twentieth century (Casper & Bianchi, 2007), and has contributed to an eroding of commitment to marriage and traditional family life. Those optimistic about the future of marriage suggest that families are not in decline, but merely changing and adapting to new socioeconomic dynamics and conditions. Those who are pessimistic suggest that the institution of marriage is a cause for concern and that divorce rates signify an increased individualism and an ending of important bonds once held together through the structure of the family (Hackstaff, 2007). The following points add to an understanding of divorce today:

- An increased emphasis on personal satisfaction and fulfillment, as a cultural shift, has made divorce a more acceptable choice for people who feel unfilled by their marriages (Bellah, Madsen, Sullivan, Swidler, & Tipton, 1985).
- Increased employment opportunities for women in the workforce have led to an increase in opportunities for women to work outside the home; this has given wives greater economic

independence and has made divorce a more attractive alternative to an unhappy marriage (Smith & Ward, 1985).

- Economic opportunities for men decreased since the early 1970s, and their reduced earning potential may have caused stress in their marriages contributing to the increase in divorce rates (Oppenheimer, 1994).
- No-fault divorce legislation from the early 1970s has made divorce an easier transaction than ever before (Rodgers, Nakonezny, & Shull, 1999).
- Divorce is more common among people with low incomes as a lack of money can cause strain and tension in a marriage (Cherlin, 1992).
- Individuals who marry as teenagers have a higher rate of divorce than those who choose partners later in life (Raley & Bumpass, 2003).
- Individuals who cohabit prior to marriage have a higher rate of divorce than those who do not, and may have a weaker commitment to marriage than people who marry without cohabitating first (Smock & Gupta, 2002).
- Children of divorce are more likely to end their own marriages in divorce, possibly modeling their behavior on their parents' marriages (Amato, 1996).
- African Americans have higher rates of marriage separation than most other racial-ethnic groups, with about one-half of the marriages of black women ending within 15 years, compared to about one-third of marriages of white women (Raley & Bumpass, 2003).
- Individuals who marry people who are similar to themselves in characteristic, such as religion, perhaps reflecting more compatibility in values and interests, have a lower rate of divorce (Lehrer & Chiswick, 1993).

Concerning the increase in divorce, Cherlin (2008) observes the following:

The great 1960s and 1970s rise in divorce probably had multiple causes: The culture was becoming more individualistic, the laws became more permissive, and women gained more economic independence through working outside the home. We can't really determine which of these factors was most important – most likely it was a combination of all of them. As for the post-1980s divergence, we don't yet know enough about it to say with confidence what has caused it. It's tempting to ascribe it to differing employment opportunities in the globalized, twenty-first century economy. The young men who have fared the worst economically are those without high school degrees, and they are the ones whose risks of divorcing have increased. In contrast, college-educated workers have fared the best, and their risks of divorce have decreased. We will need more research on this topic. . . . (p. 413)

Divorce can have a profound impact on all lives involved and can have both long-term and short-term negative effects on children. In the long term, divorce raises the risk for children from divorce environments of dropping out of high school, bearing a child before marriage, or suffering from mental health problems as an adult. In the short term, it leaves the household split, taking away a system and environment of full support for the child and the child's development. This reduction in help and monitoring can leave children without important needs being met. And, the remaining or custodial parent may hold negative views regarding the divorce, further negatively impacting the environment in which the child is living. The child may suffer by being caught in a conflict between two parents who are unhappy with each other, and an increased number of different and challenging transitions. Significant and lasting problems in personal relationships have been identified with children of divorce (Wallerstein & Blakeslee, 1989; Wallerstein, Lewis, & Blakeslee, 2000).

Increasing numbers of children today are being raised in divorced families, stepparent families, and families where both parents work outside the home. As divorce rates have increased, a significant number of children are being raised in single-parent families. The United States has a higher percentage of single-parent families than virtually any other industrialized country. About one in every four children in the United States by age 18 has lived a portion of their lives in a stepfamily; more than two of every three mothers with a child from six to seventeen years of age are in the workforce (Santrock, 2008). Regardless of the difficulties for children brought about by divorce, support from relatives, friends, and others, an ongoing positive relationship between the custodial parent and the ex-spouse, the ability to meet financial needs, and quality schooling can help children adjust to the stressful circumstances of divorce (Huurree, Junkkari, & Aro, 2006).

Remarriage and Stepfamilies

Historically, most remarriages have come following the death of a spouse. This has changed, however, with the decline in adult death rates in the twentieth century and the increase in divorce. Nine in ten remarriages in the United States today follow a divorce, as opposed to a death. Over forty percent of weddings in the United States represent a remarriage for one or both of the individuals involved (U.S. National Center for Health Statistics, 1991). Women who marry at a younger age are more likely to marry again than women who marry at an older age, perhaps due to their having had less experience and preference for living alone (Bumpass, Sweet, & Martin, 1990). Additionally, women who divorce at a younger age are more likely to remarry than those who divorce at an older age (Bramlet & Mosher, 2002).

Rates of remarriage are lower for those from lower rather than higher socioeconomic levels. Bramlett and Mosher (2002) identify that remarriage is more likely among non-Hispanic whites than among Hispanics or African Americans. Lower remarriage rates for African Americans are consistent with the lesser place of marriage in the African American family. Fewer African Americans become married in the first place.

Remarriages that involve children from a previous marriage create situations where new rules about everyday family life need to be established. Following a divorce, children typically reside with one parent, usually the mother. While the rate of remarriage has fallen since the 1960s among divorced persons, the rate of cohabitation has risen. The growth of childbearing outside of marriage and cohabitation suggest an expanded definition of stepfamilies that includes households where two adults are married or cohabitating, and at least one child from a previous marriage or relationship. A clear stressor in this relationship is that courts typically give legal priority to the biological parent who resides outside the home as a result of the divorce over a stepparent who lives with the child in the family. This circumstance and other dynamics often cause the stepparent, even though residing in the home, to be more of an outsider than an insider in the family. The impact of this type of situation can be particularly difficult for children. Hetherington and Clingempeel (1992) identify that children in stepfamilies or single-parent households show lower levels of well-being in terms of behavior and more adjustment problems than children in two-biological-parent families. Too, children in stepfamilies tend to move out of their households at an earlier age than children in single-parent or two-parent households (Coleman, Ganong, & Fine, 2000).

Domestic Violence and Child Abuse

Domestic violence has been a social issue in the United States from early colonial days. Domestic violence can be seen in minor as well as major injuries, attempts to coerce through acts such as slapping or through the threat of injury, and stalking, even if actual physical violence does not occur. A broad definition of domestic violence may be found in viewing it through a political perspective. From the political perspective, it is seen in the relations of power and authority between men and women. This view suggests that domestic violence is grounded in laws and customs that have and continue to support male dominance and is not likely to be stopped without political action. From a medical view, domestic violence is seen as an illness.

Although some women engage in domestic violence, women are far more often the victims than the aggressors. The National Violence Against Women Survey by the National Institute of Justice and the Centers for Disease Control and Prevention, between November 1995 and May 1996, reported 22 percent of women surveyed identified that they had been the victims of physical assault by an intimate partner; 18 percent had been pushed, grabbed, or shoved; 16 percent had been slapped or hit; and 9 percent had had their hair pulled and had been beaten up (Cherlin 2008). Eight percent of women reported having been raped or having experienced an attempted rape by an intimate partner (U.S. National Institute of Justice, 2006). Sexual violence is often linked to physical violence and studies have shown that forced sexual acts tend to occur in violent marriages. Such problems are more common among cohabitating couples than among married couples (Stets & Straus, 1989; U.S. National Institute of Justice, 2000). Although domestic violence can be seen in all social classes, higher rates can be found among low-income rather than middle-income couples (Sorenson, Upchurch, & Shen, 1996; U.S. Bureau of Justice Statistics, 1995). Research shows that domestic violence can be found across cultures.

Most consider that domestic assaults arise, in part, from power struggles between men and women. Men generally have an advantage in these struggles because of their greater physical strength, and because of a social system that tends to reinforce male dominance. It is popularly felt that children from violent homes learn that violent behavior is an acceptable and often effective means of controlling others and are more likely, as adults, to use violence against a spouse and children. Most people calculate the rewards and costs of violent behavior, and the alternatives to it; women who have some economic resources and potential for independence are less likely than others who do not have such resources and potential to be victimized.

With respect to child abuse, Straus and Stewart (1999) identify that hitting children is the most tolerated form of family violence and that nearly all parents slap or spank their children at some point. In its most common definition, however, child abuse is serious physical harm (e.g., trauma, sexual abuse with injury, or willful malnutrition) with intent to injure. Studies through the National Incidence Study of Child Abuse and Neglect (U.S. Department of Health and Human Services, 2003) report that the percentage of substantiated cases of child abuse and/or neglect include: 60 percent neglect, 20 percent physical abuse, 10 percent sexual abuse, and approximately 8 percent emotional abuse. More than half of the reports reflect parental neglect, not abuse, with more than half of the neglect cases representing educational neglect, which typically means that the children weren't attending school regularly. Child abuse is not found equally in all families, but is seen more in low-income families, single-parent families, and families where husbands do not have a full-time job (Sedlak & Broadhurst, 1996; Steinmetz, 1987).

Low-income parents are more likely to use physical punishment and criticize their children harshly than parents from middle to high income levels (McLoyd, Aikens, & Burton, 2006). Although the reports of child neglect and abuse have increased greatly in recent decades, the increase may reflect more complete reporting rather than an actual increase in rates. In the late 1980s and 1990s, the number of children in foster care rose dramatically. Nevertheless, there is continued debate about whether government social programs should emphasize the preservation of families or the protection of children. This is a discussion that is not likely to result in agreement and closure in the near future.

Family and Social Policy

Debate continues over the role of government in families and the impact that social policy changes have had on families and their status in the United States. Much of this debate and divergence of opinion is broken down along conservative and liberal thinking lines. Numerous programs were established in the twentieth century to offer support for individuals and families, the most notable being the Social Security Act of 1935, under President Franklin Delano Roosevelt, and Aid to Families with Dependent Children (AFDC). These programs, which virtually established modern day welfare reform, have had tremendous impact on the development of families as well as overall economic conditions in the United States. More recently, under President Bill Clinton, Congress passed the Personal Responsibility and Work Opportunity Reconciliation Act (PRWORA) in 1996 that dramatically changed those conditions under which individuals might receive government support. These reforms have greatly expanded, and redefined, the government's assistance role to families.

The lines between conservative and liberal thinking in terms of assisting children and families, however, are not always easy to identify. Generally, conservatives believe that the government should not be involved, or less involved, in family matters. Regardless, the government has been involved in family matters in areas ranging from family support, to tax programs, to promoting marriage, to abortion. To conservatives, one of the most visible causes of the fragmentation of the family has been government welfare payments, which, to many, have made fatherless families a viable option (Giele, 2007). A second cause has been secularization and the decline of religious affiliations that have, again to many, undermined the norms of sexual abstinence before marriage and the prohibitions of adultery and divorce. The solution to a breakdown in family values, to conservatives, is to revitalize and reinstitutionalize marriage.

Contrarily, liberal views focus more on utilizing government to help families. Measures have been enacted to help married couples where wives are employed outside the home, and single parents, rather than help breadwinner-homemaker couples. Assisting families through child-care and day-care programs, and programs where parents may stay at home to care for their children, are other examples of more liberal-oriented thinking. While liberals concur that there are problems in America's families, such as in health care and in the conditions of children, they identify the primary issues causing these problems being economic and societal changes that have brought about new demands on the family without providing appropriate social supports (Giele, 2007). The dramatic changes in the family are due to the advent of the money economy, rather than cultural and moral decline, as is often identified by conservatives.

Bringing renewed debate between conservatives and liberals was the 1996 PRWORA federal legislation that authorized states to set a time limit of five years, or less, on the receipt of cash assistance through Temporary Assistance for Needy Families (TANF). It also specified that employment be sought, and required, to alter the entitlement mentality for low-income single-parent families that had become a large part of government welfare assistance. Conservative supporters of the legislation take the position that dependence on public benefits is counter to the health of low-income families, where liberals identify that such dependence is actually a symptom of the country's poverty problem.

Issues surrounding heterosexual marriage and same-sex marriage also abound in social and governmental arenas and also can be divided on conservative and liberal lines as well. Congress' passage of welfare reform legislation in 2006, that included a program that provided the states with significant financial incentives to promote heterosexual marriage, came only after considerable debate and division. Included were issues of politics, diversity, morality, and economics. The increased debate surrounding same-sex marriage is projected to continue. Though same-sex marriage is legal in Massachusetts and Canada, some states have enacted constitutional amendments against it. The Defense of Marriage Act (DOMA) of 1996, noted earlier, is an example of government action intended to reinforce a particular definition of marriage and, thus, family. How developments such as these impact the family in the long run is yet to be seen. Questions raised by conservatives, liberals, gays, feminists, and others will be prominent in how families develop in the future.

THE AMERICAN FAMILY – THE FUTURE

There is no reason to believe that the ongoing changes to, and in the view of some the challenges to, the American family will subside in the foreseeable future. What is clear is that the definition of family will not return to that which was found in earlier times. If the past fifty to sixty years are any indication, much more change and transition are yet to come. It also may be anticipated that the 2008 presidential election in the United States will include special attention given to the political role and government influence in various areas of America's family life such as support for individuals in low socioeconomic situations, welfare reform, health care, child care, and education. However, it also could include different ways to look at the overall definition of family in terms of heterosexual marriages, same-sex marriages, single-parent homes, etc. It certainly will further accent the differences between liberal and conservative philosophy.

As values continue to change, and as the United States continues to be a more and more diverse society, culturally, economically, religiously, etc., the differing views that come forward to touch all aspects of American life will influence future directions and definitions of the family. One might accept that the divisions already drawn between conservative and liberal thinking will remain strongly in place. Family watchers, in particular those in fields such as sociology, psychology, education, health, political science, philosophy, and business and economics, will have ample opportunity to observe developments in this area. Regardless, it is clear that the traditional definition of family, to some immortalized in the *Ozzie and Harriet* and *Leave it to Beaver* television programs of the 1950s and 1960s, most assuredly is no more.

REFERENCES

Amato, P. (2001). Children of divorce in the 1990s: An update of the Amato and Keith (1991) meta-analysis. *Journal of Family Psychology, 15,* 355–370.

Amato, P. (1996). Explaining the intergenerational transmission of divorce. *Journal of Marriage and the Family, 58* (628–640).

Bellah, R., Madsen, R., Sullivan, W., Swidler, A., & Tipton, S. (1985). *Habits of the heart: Individualism and commitment in America.* Berkeley, CA: University of California Press.

Berk, L. (2005). *Infants, children, and adolescents* (5th ed.). Boston: Allyn and Bacon.

Bramlett, M., & Mosher, W. (2002). *Cohabitation, marriage, divorce, and remarriage in the United States.* www.cdc.gov/nchs/data/series/sr_23/sr23_022.pdf.

Bumpass, L., Sweet, J., & Martin, T. (1990). Changing patterns of remarriage. *Journal of Marriage and Family, 52,* 747–756.

Casper L., & Bianchi, S. (2007). Cohabitation. In A. Skolnick & J. Skolnick (Eds.), *Family in transition* (14th ed.). Boston: Allyn & Bacon.

Cherlin, A. (1992). *Marriage, divorce, remarriage.* Cambridge, MA: Harvard University Press.

Cherlin, A. (2008). *Public and private families: An introduction* (5th ed.). Boston: McGraw Hill.

Coleman, M., Ganong, L., & Fine, M. (2000). Reinvestigating remarriage: Another decade of progress. *Journal of Marriage and Family, 62,* 1288–1307.

Giele, J. (2007). Decline of the family: Conservative, liberal, and feminist views. In A. Skolnick & J. Skolnick (Eds.), *Family in transition* (14th ed.). Boston: Allyn & Bacon.

Glendon, M. (1987). *Abortion and divorce in Western law.* Cambridge, MA: Harvard University Press.

Goode, W. (2007). The theoretical importance of the family. In A. Skolnick & J. Skolnick (Eds.), *Family in transition* (14th ed.). Boston: Allyn & Bacon.

Hackstaff, K. (2007). Divorce culture: A quest for relational equality in marriage. In A. Skolnick & J. Skolnick (Eds.), *Family in transition* (14th ed.). Boston: Allyn & Bacon.

Hernandez, D. (2007). Changes in demographics of families over the course of American history. In A. Skolnick & J. Skolnick (Eds.), *Family in transition* (14th ed.). Boston: Allyn & Bacon.

Hetherington, E., & Clingempeel, G. (1992). Coping with marital transition. *Monographs of the Society for Research in Child Development, 57.*

Huurree, T., Junkkari, H., & Aro, H. (2006). Long-term psychological effects of parental divorce: A follow-up study from adolescence to adult. *European Archives of Psychiatry and Clinical Neuroscience,* 256–263.

Lehrer, E., & Chiswick, C. (1993). Religion as a determinant of marital stability. *Demography, 30,* 385–404.

McLoyd, V., Aikens, N., & Burton, L. (2006). Childhood poverty, policy, and practice. In W. Damon & R. Lerner (Eds.), *Handbook of child psychology* (6th ed.). New York: Wiley.

Oppenheimer, V. (1994). Women's rising employment and the future of the family in industrial societies. *Population and Developmental Review, 20,* 203–342.

Phillips, R. (1991). *Untying the knot: A short history of divorce.* Cambridge, England: Cambridge University Press.

Raley, R., & Bumpass, I. (2003). The topography of the divorce plateau: Levels and trends in union stability in the United States after 1980. *Demographic Research, 8,* 245–259.

Rodgers, J., Nakonezny, P., & Shull, R. (1999). Did no-fault divorce legislation matter? Definitely yes and sometimes no. *Journal of Marriage and the Family, 61,* 803–809.

Santrock, J. (2008). *Educational psychology* (3rd ed.). Boston: McGraw Hill.

Skolnick, A., & Skolnick, J. (2007). *Family in transition* (14th ed.). Boston: Allyn and Bacon.

Sedlak, A., & Broadhurst, D. (1996). *Executive summary of the third national incidence study of child abuse and neglect.* Washington, DC: National Center on Child Abuse and Neglect, Administration for Children and Families, U.S. Department of Health and Human Services.

Smith, J., & Ward, M. (1985). Time-series growth in the female labor force. *Journal of Labor Economics, 3*, 859–890.

Smock, P., & Gupta, S. (2002). Cohabitation in contemporary North America. In A. Booth & A.C. Crouter (Eds.), *Just living together: Implications for cohabitation on families, children, and social policy* (pp. 53–84). Mahwah, NJ: Earlbaum.

Sorenson, S., Upchurch, D., & Shen, H. (1996). Violence and injury in marital arguments: Risk patterns and gender differences. *American Journal of Public Health, 86*, 35–40.

Steinmetz, S. (1987). Family violence: Past, present, and future. In M.B. Sussman & S. K. Steinmetz (Eds.), *Handbook of marriage and the family*. New York: Plenum Press.

Stets, J., & Straus, M. (1989). The marriage as a hitting license: A comparison of assault in dating, cohabiting and married couples. In M.A. Pirog-Good & J.E. Stets (Eds.), *Violence in dating relationships*. New York: Praeger.

Straus, M., & Stewart, J. (1999). Corporal punishment by American parents. *Clinical Child and Family Psychology Review, 2*, 55–70.

Thorne, B. (1992). Feminist rethinking of the family: An overview. In B. Thorne & M. Yalom (Eds.), *Rethinking the family: Some feminist questions* (Rev. ed.). Boston: Northeastern University Press.

U.S. Bureau of Justice Statistics. (1995). *Violence against women: Estimates from the redesigned survey* (NCJ 154348). Washington, DC: U.S. Government Printing Office.

U.S. Department of Health and Human Services. (2003). *Child maltreatment 2001.* http://www.acf.hhs.gov.

U.S. National Center for Health Statistics. (1991). *Advance report of final marriage statistics, 1988* (Monthly Vital Statistics Report 40, No. 4 Supplement). Washington, DC: U.S. Government Printing Office.

U.S. National Institute of Justice. (2000). *Extent, nature and consequences of intimate partner violence* (No. NCJ 181867).

U.S. National Institute of Justice. (2006). *Extent, nature, and consequences of rape victimization: Findings from the national violence against women survey.* http://www.ncjrs.gov.

Wallerstein, J., & Blakeslee, S. (1989). *Second chances: Men, women, and children in a decade after divorce.* New York: Ticknor and Fields.

Wallerstein, J., Lewis, J., & Blakeslee, S. (2000). *The unexpected legacy of divorce.* New York: Hyperion.

Chapter 2

WHAT IS "FAMILY"? DEFINING THE TERMS OF THE U.S. WELFARE STATE

Holley E. Tankersley

The promotion of "family values" has dominated political rhetoric in the United States for nearly sixty years. Politicians use this ambiguous term to appeal to voters' perceived desires for a return to an American past in which social and economic life was less complicated. Ironically, the introduction of family values into the political debate is anything but simple; the use of the term makes politics vastly more complicated, as it is widely accepted that the word "values" is an inherently political term with ideological connotations. While both Republican and Democratic Party candidates claim to carry the mantle of traditional American values, they most certainly define those values in different ways. The vagaries of electoral politics consequently result in one definition of values dominating the nature of public policy for the duration of the official's term in office. Indeed, the struggle over whose ideologically defined values should guide American politics and public policy is generally considered the source of nearly all domestic political conflict.

Less present in the public policy or political debate, but perhaps just as controversial, is the definition of "family." The majority of social welfare and labor policies in the United States incorporate at least a handful of provisions that either rely on or recognize alternate definitions of family when delineating eligibility for benefits. Consequently, it becomes critical to define "family" in such a way that meets the realities of modern life. If policymakers operate on outdated or ideological definitions of family, they will design policies that are ultimately inconsistent with contemporary social structures. These policies will inevitably be ineffective and, in the worst case scenario, produce undesirable social outcomes. Piven and Cloward (1987) note that the social welfare state is a secondary institution serving the needs of primary institutions: government and the economy. As such, social policy must promote both political and economic legitimacy. However, if these goals are in service of primary institutions, then family might be considered a primary institution as well. After all, politicians have implied that "family values" will strengthen both civil society and the economy.

If we are to design a viable and functioning set of public policies, we must first define the family to which the social welfare state is in service. Defining "family," then, becomes critical not just for the formation and implementation of public policy, but for an understanding of the evolution of normative ideals of American society and economy.

"FAMILY" AND FAMILY POLICY

There are no less than ten formal English-language definitions for the word "family." While more traditional definitions of family are driven by considerations of binding ties of blood, adoption, and marriage, policymakers have also included technical considerations such as the pooling and distribution of income and resources across individuals and households (Hill, 1995; Smith, 1993). Thus "family" may be considered both a social and economic construct, equally important in both civil society and the free market. Consequently, policies that impact family formation and well-being are quite widespread and diverse. Policies governing income taxes, child and dependent care, health care, child support, public assistance, Social Security, family leave, equal opportunity employment, and family planning are all derived from assumptions about what comprises a family and which of those family types is entitled to receive specific benefits from the state (Hill, 1995).

Within the study of the social welfare state, these policies are examined under the rubric of "family policy." Family policy is simply the response of any government to the problems and needs of the family, or government actions that will have more than a negligible effect on families (Monroe, 1995). This distinct sphere of public policymaking began to emerge in the post-World War II period as interest in post-materialism and postmodern policy design developed, and its evolution has continued apace. Indeed, the U.S. Congress has been consistently active in family policy-making since the midpoint of the twentieth century; family policy legislation has been introduced in every single Congress since 1945, resulting in the drafting and sponsorship of more than 5000 bills between 1945 and 2005 (Burstein et al., 1995; U.S. House, 2007; U.S. Senate, 2007).

While the policymaking process for most U.S. domestic policies (especially economic, environmental, and education policies) is dominated by rational analysis, social learning, and empirical knowledge, family policy, like the debate over values, is driven primarily by ideological battles. Indeed, the struggle to define "family" has produced three general debates that continue to shape family policy (Rayman & Bookman, 1999):

1. Is there only one valid type of family structure? Can non-traditional families create the same sort of social stability that has been attributed to traditional family structures and values?
2. Should family be a dynamic construct that reflects real social, economic, and demographic changes, or should family be a static construct that guides the development of future values and public policies?
3. What are the proper gender roles and the place of both men and women in the family and the workplace? Can the state avoid defining these roles in its creation of both family and labor policy?

While the political and policy debate is unlikely to produce a universally satisfactory answer to any of these questions, the attempt to divine such answers can provide a deeper understanding of the importance of family to both society and the state.

The "Valid" Family: Normative Definitions and Family Policy

The most popular traditional construct of "family" in the United States consists of a coresident nuclear unit headed by opposite sex married partners with minor children. The male spouse takes on the role of primary breadwinner; death is the typical reason for his exit from the family (Hill, 1995). In the strictest interpretation of this arrangement, women are not expected to participate in the private labor force. This traditional definition became dominant during the 1930s and 1940s, the period of history that saw a new American social welfare state spring almost whole from the foreheads of Franklin Roosevelt and his New Deal policy advisors. In addition to the development of what is still the framework for modern social policy, a significant portion of economic and labor policy was also developed during this time period. As a result, notes sociologist Martha Hill, "The general premise underscoring social support policies [was] that public policies should buffer families from economic hardship by protecting the main breadwinner from serious labor market difficulties (e.g., unemployment, low wages, retirement with inadequate pension funds) or ensuring an income flow to young children or elderly women who had lost their main breadwinner to death" (1995, 37).

Despite its dominance, the notion of a coresident nuclear family as the normative family structure in the U.S. only dates back to the industrial period of American history. Prior to the period of the industrial revolution, extended-family households were the normative ideal (Rayman & Bookman, 1999). Economic necessity mandated that multiple generations live together in order to successfully manage the family farm or the family business in an agrarian and local or regional trade market (Smith, 1993). The more family members who coresided, the better off the family would be in economic terms, having created a sort of familial economy of scale. However, the industrialization of the U.S. economy eliminated the need for extended families to coreside and participate jointly in economic activities. Corporations promised more job security and real income; Roosevelt pledged state support for labor unions and labor laws; and the new linkage between private economic activity and social insurance (both Social Security and disability benefits) ensured the availability of a social safety net for industrial workers. From the 1930s forward, nuclear families became the standard unit of analysis for economic and social policy, and families and private sector employers became inextricably linked. Because of the critical nature of this linkage, the traditional nuclear coresident definition of family was transformed from the modal structure to the most-desirable structure – the one that the state and industry encouraged individuals to create and maintain.

The traditional definition of family as a coresident, nuclear unit was reemphasized by the U.S. Congress in both 1993 and 1996. The Family Medical and Leave Act of 1993 (FMLA) mandates that employers provide employees with leave from work in order to cope with personal illness, to care for a sick family member, or to care for a new son or daughter. Employers are expected to protect the employee's job and to continue to extend benefits throughout the duration of the leave. For the purposes of the FMLA, the Congress defines family as a spouse, son, daughter, or parent, but does not specify residential arrangements. A son or daughter is further defined as a biological child or a child brought into the family via adoption, foster care, marriage (i.e., stepchildren), legal guardianship, or *in loco parentis* status. The term "spouse" was defined in the Defense of Marriage Act of 1996 (DOMA). The DOMA was intended to clarify the U.S. government's position toward homosexual marriage; as such, it stated that the formal definition of spouse is a husband or wife of opposite sex from his or her partner. Again, the DOMA did not make reference to coresidency.

Considering the historical development of the notion of "family," including the industrialization of the U.S. economy, the establishment of a modern social welfare state in the 1930s, and modern legislation that explicitly defines family for the purposes of eligibility for benefits, most research and policymaking in the family policy arena is currently guided by a handful of major assumptions (Hill, 1995). First, "family" is defined as it was during the New Deal era, as a nuclear unit consisting of a husband, wife, and minor children. Second, the husband/father is expected to be the primary breadwinner, while the female spouse is a nonparticipant in the labor force, especially before the minor children reach school age. Third, the most likely reason for the loss of the male breadwinner is death. Fourth, only those individuals who coreside are considered part of the nuclear family. Finally, family members are expected to pool and share social and economic resources. Despite the longevity of these assumptions, or perhaps because of it, contemporary scholars have recently begun to challenge the traditional definition of family that has driven family policy for the last sixty years. Indeed, new sociological, demographic, and policy analysis suggests that family, as both a social and economic construct, is a dynamic concept, the definition of which must be altered to fit the needs of modern American citizens and civil society.

Family as a Dynamic Construct

Demographic and sociological research suggests that the policy assumptions that developed from a normative definition of family in the latter half of the twentieth century are no longer valid. The modal definition of family in the United States can no longer support these heroic assumptions because American family structures underwent significant changes between 1960 and 1980. While coresident nuclear units continued to be both the modal situation and the normative ideal of family, increases in divorce rates, changing rates of female house-holders, and an increase in nonmarital births began to alter the reality of family life and the utility of existing family policy (Eggebeen & Lichter, 1991).

Between 1960 and 2006, the divorce rate for adult males (aged 15+) increased by 78 percent, while the rate for adult females increased by 75 percent in the same period (U.S. Census, 2007). For women aged 30–59, divorce is the most common reason for the loss of a spouse; indeed, by 2006, divorce was responsible for 40 percent of spousal loss compared to 5 percent for death (Hill, 1995). There has also been an increase in the birth rate for unmarried mothers from 5.3 percent in 1960 to 36.8 percent in 2005 (ChildTrends). Consequently, 25 percent of minor children in the U.S. do not live in a coresident nuclear family. This specific change to family structure may also be the secondary result of the increase in divorce rates. Women who experienced divorce in a first marriage have a 75 percent likelihood of remarrying within ten years of marital dissolution; men remarry at a higher rate (approximately 80 percent) and remarry more quickly than do women (Bramlett & Mosher, 2001). As a result, 40 percent of adult men in their thirties and forties have minor children living elsewhere, and nearly 65 percent of those men have minor stepchildren to support in their new marital households (Hill, 1995).

Taken together, these changes present a unique problem for family policymakers: the bulk of U.S. social and family policy was developed on the premise that the state should provide support for mothers after the death of a spouse, who was assumed to be the primary breadwinner in the coresident nuclear family. The problem is especially evident in public assistance (previously known as Aid to Families with Dependent Children (AFDC) and now called Temporary Assistance to Needy Families (TANF)), which was designed upon the now archaic premise that loss of the main breadwinner (to death) would cause economic hardship that the state could alleviate by helping another family member, presumably the mother, to step in and support the family (Hill, 1995; Oliker, 1994). The original version of this policy granted eligibility for the receipt of welfare support to widows with the goal of helping them to maintain their status as full-time homemakers. Indeed, eligibility was confined to widowed women with children and no coresident male. Considering the reality of current marriage and birth statistics, this policy focus on widows with children is sorely out-dated and misplaced.

In cases where the primary breadwinner is lost to divorce – the more common situation today – a more suitable and effective family policy is one that forces a transfer of funds from the absent breadwin-ner to dependent members of the family (i.e., child support, alimony, etc.). The policy focus effectively shifts from state funded social wel-fare programs to mandatory private transfers governed by family law. In light of the increase in non-marital births, policymakers might also choose to refocus their efforts on any number of policies, from family planning to job training and workforce planning to family leave and workplace flexibility. Whichever focus is chosen as the better alterna-tive, it is critical that policymakers continue to make pragmatic adjust-ments based on the new reality of American families instead of adher-ing to the old normative ideal of coresident nuclear families. If the pragmatic approach does not lead to a shift in policy, family policy itself will result in ineffective, or perhaps harmful, outcomes.

In addition to changes in marriage and births, there have been sig-nificant changes to the nature of coresidency. Coresidents may not be "family members" in the traditional nuclear sense, but may function as a family structure for economic and partnership purposes. These fam-ilies may include homosexual partners, non-married heterosexual partners, or extended family members. According to the U.S. Census Bureau, 10 to 20 percent of individuals across all age and gender groups reside with someone other than a nuclear family member. Un-married partner households numbered more than 5 million in 2006, approximately 5 percent of the total U.S. households (U.S. Census Bureau, 2007). Additionally, 5 percent of adults over the age of 40 are the primary caregivers for their grandchildren (U.S. Census Bureau, 2007). Individuals in these nonnuclear yet coresident households may desire to support their coresidents with their health benefits, social insurance benefits, or other state provided income. Several industrialized democracies, including France and Canada, allow individuals beyond a parent, child, or spouse to apply for benefits that would allow them to care for a coresident partner in cases of illness or death. However, the bulk of current U.S. policy operates under a definition of "family" or kinship that would not support such official transfers.

Gender Roles, Economic Considerations, and Family Policy

The third major debate that shapes both the definition of family and the content of family policy in the U.S. concerns the level of state involvement in defining or promoting traditional gender roles in both family and work life. Sapiro (1990) notes that the majority of social and family policies that specifically benefit women have been designed to "explicitly benefit [women] in their capacity as wives and mothers" (1990, 44). This presents a particular theoretical dilemma: it effectively dismisses the possibility that a woman could be the primary breadwinner, thus implying that the woman is a dependent who does not need the education, training, or government support that would enable her to become the primary breadwinner. Rather, she needs either direct support from a coresident male or indirect support via household transfers from a former coresident male. Existing social and family policy, therefore, reinforces traditional gender roles both in the family and the workplace, regardless of marital status.

Why does this situation persist in a modern democratic state with a capitalist economy? Put simply, policies that would enable women to successfully support their children without a spouse's income undermine the traditional definition of family that has governed U.S. policy since the 1940s. More conservative citizens and politicians view this as a threat to traditional social standards, a viewpoint that has only been strengthened by the "feminization of poverty" thesis (Pearce, 1978), which suggests that female householders are more likely to lead poor or low socioeconomic status families. This creates a policy atmosphere in which female-headed families, especially those in which a husband is not present, are treated as deviant structures in need of paternalistic government assistance (Hill, 1995). Interestingly, the traditional definition of family also precludes lower-income single males from obtaining social assistance, thus undermining the efforts of many fathers to provide for their children, regardless of whether the father is the head of the child's household. If family was defined on biological terms rather than being tied to marriage and/or coresidence, fathers would remain eligible for welfare state assistance and be better able to transfer income to their minor children.

While the theoretical underpinnings of traditional definitions of family appear to relegate women to nonparticipation in the labor force, actual legislation regarding gender responsibilities and workforce participation has been driven by post-World War II social and economic realities. Despite the ideological or rhetorical desire to maintain traditional social standards, the breathtaking change in family structure and family roles has prompted a significant evolution of social and economic policy. Much of this change has been driven by the increase in women working outside of the home. Labor force participation of women has increased from 31 percent in 1949 to 75 percent in 1999; the percentage of full-time female homemakers dropped dramatically during the same time period, from almost 70 percent to only 15 percent (Rayman & Bookman, 1999; U.S. Census Bureau, 2007).

The U.S. Congress appears to have adjusted policy to meet this reality. Burstein, Bricher, and Einwoher (1995) studied congressional sponsorships of legislation concerning work, family, and gender. They classified congressional sponsorships into three different spheres, each of which reflects a different definition of "family." The first, "separate spheres," encompasses the view that women should not enter the public sphere of paid work. This clearly adheres to the most traditional definition of family. Legislation supporting "separate spheres" would restrict women's access to the labor market, permit differential pay on the basis of family status or gender, and limit paid work in the home (Burstein et al., 1995).

The second sphere of legislation is the "equal opportunity" sphere. This group of policies represents the belief that women should have the same job opportunities as men, but traditional gender roles in the family should remain intact (Burstein et al., 1995). For example, these policies would require equal opportunity and equal pay, but would encourage women to work less than full-time, provide benefits to the male worker only, and provide parental leave to female, but not male, employees. The final sphere, "work-family accommodation," holds that family and paid work cannot be separated (Burstein et al., 1995). In this view, employers should be subject to regulations that require them to accommodate leave for dependent care for both male and female employees. It would support differential time at paid work, permit paid work in the home, and give all employees control over work hours for the explicit purpose of caring for children.

The results of the congressional analysis revealed that political support for work-family accommodation has increased significantly from the 1980s to present (Burstein et al., 1995). Since 1945, 15 percent of sponsorships were for separate spheres bills, 59 percent for equal opportunity, and 23 percent were work-family accommodation bills. Moreover, discernible trends in support for these policy ideas have emerged over time. In the post–World War II period, most legislation was geared towards separate spheres bills as society embraced the idea of a return to prewar social structures. However, there was a quick turnaround once politicians (and corporate executives) realized that women were determined to stay in the work force. The postwar focus quickly turned to equal opportunity. Twenty-nine laws supporting equal opportunity were passed between 1945 and 1990, while none of the separate spheres bills made it through the entire legislative process. It was during the 1980s that work-family accommodation bills truly increased in popularity and dominance. Between 1981 and 1990, nine accommodation bills had hearings and two were signed into law; this represented an increase of 56 percent. These bills required employers to be gender-neutral in questions of child support, retirement, and other issues, and to provide leave to parents for sick-care of children. During the same time period (1981–1990), the percentage of separate spheres bills declined precipitously (63%). Support for equal opportunity policies has remained steady over time (Burstein et al., 1995).

It is unclear why policymakers have been willing to alter policy that combines elements of family and work, while they seem unwilling to make concomitant changes in policies relating to the changing nature of marriage, childbearing, and household composition. Perhaps the former are more important to the state, as they fulfill the pragmatic purpose of helping to maintain the overall health of the economy, while the latter are more controversial ideological issues. Indeed, it is clear that support for diverse packages of work, family, and gender policies rises and falls according to changing realities of roles and responsibilities within the family. It becomes pragmatic for the state to sponsor work-family accommodation bills as the percentage of single-parent families increases. It also becomes pragmatic to make policy adjustments as the market increasingly requires both parents to work outside of the home, a development of the postindustrial service economy, which has reduced the number of lower-skilled jobs that pay a family wage (Schram, 1992). If the government failed to make these policy changes, it would be faced with an increase in the number of families requiring social welfare support, thereby increasing state obligations.

SYMBOLIC POLICYMAKING, DIVERSITY, AND THE ROLE OF THE STATE

Several additional points of controversy infuse the three major debates over the definition of "family" and the direction of family policy. The first is the question of whether elected officials properly incorporate the realities of family life into family policy, or whether their policies are simply created to perpetuate the normative ideal of the traditional family structure. The Family Support Act of 1988 (FSA) is a classic example of policymakers' tendency to legislate symbolically rather than responsibly. Sociologists and policy analysts on both ends of the ideological spectrum "rediscovered" poverty in the 1970s and early 1980s. William Julius Wilson (1987) and Charles Murray (1984) both published books of significant and controversial research exploring the linkages between family structure, poverty, human behavior and incentives, and the need for public assistance. The increased interest in such research, combined with bloated federal budgets, negative popular perceptions of welfare and welfare recipients, and Ronald Reagan's rhetoric of retrenchment, led Congress to seek reform of public assistance policy (Oliker, 1994).

The FSA was actually lauded for its bipartisan, non-ideological nature. Conservatives were most interested in ensuring the Act's focus on work and education requirements for those receiving welfare assistance, and liberals wanted to include support services that remove the barriers to work (e.g., child care assistance, transportation, training) that most often prevent women from entering the labor force. While these provisions were based on solid research suggesting them as policy alternatives to reduce welfare dependency, the legislation that was passed and signed into law was designed to address popular perceptions of the failure of welfare policies rather than the actual causes of those failures (Oliker, 1994; Piven & Cloward, 1987; Sapiro, 1990; Schram, 1992). The FSA had three major elements: a JOBS program that required mothers receiving AFDC to complete high school, seek additional education, or enter the workforce; extensions of child care and health care benefits up to one year after exiting the welfare rolls; and a six-month extension of aid to two-parent families where the male parent was unemployed, a clear effort to encourage the mainte-nance of traditional, two-parent families. However, the FSA was less about helping families than it was about addressing the negative per-ceptions of welfare and welfare recipients. Exclusion of the male par-ent from welfare eligibility (the standard policy before the FSA) pro-vided single mothers with support but undermined traditional notions of family. Yet, providing two-parent families with more support argu-ably targeted assistance to those who needed less help. Even if one parent in the family is nonparticipant in the labor force, he or she could provide a family resource such as child care or transportation assistance to the working parent. Why would such a policy exist if po-liticians were truly concerned with reducing the costs of public assis-tance? As Sanford Schram suggests, "extending aid only to single-par-ent families encourages the breakup of poor families, while extending aid to two-parent families would theoretically alleviate this problem" (1992, 647).

The second controversy that plagues family policy is the question of race. Research suggests that definitions of "family" should vary by race, as the proportion of nonmarital births and single-motherhood has increased more rapidly among black women (Eggebeen & Lichter, 1991; Hill, 1995). Indeed, Wilson (1987) and Murray (1984) both agree that the deterioration of the nuclear family structure among lower income black families has led directly to the divergence of the pro-portion of black and white families who fall beneath the poverty line. Rayman and Bookman (1999) make the argument that the state has placed such a high value on the traditional, coresident nuclear family structure that society now perceives diverse families, with diversity defined by race and ethnicity, to be much less competent at raising children and providing stability and support for all family members. More recently, political leaders have extended this argument to homo-sexual partners who wish to marry and have or adopt children. Any family structure outside of the traditional norm is, therefore, devalued in the eyes of policymakers, and is thus subject to paternalistic treat-ment.

Finally, debates over family and family policy are infused with questions about whether matters of family and family structure should even be a matter of public or government intervention and whether the state has the ability to effectively modify behavior in the realm of family matters. The rhetorical benefit of highlighting "family values" or traditional family structures is most often associated with American conservatives. The neoconservative reaction to the rise of the "New Left" during the 1960s led to a particularly strong emphasis on traditional family values during the 1980s. It was during this period that conservatives became standard bearers for the family policy theme, perfecting the use of pro-family values rhetoric that implies a preference for traditional, male-dominated families. This preference manifested itself in a clear policy agenda. Conservatives have been at the forefront of political efforts to scale back or eliminate support for single-parent families, encourage and support marriage, and prevent homosexual unions and limit the parental rights of homosexual couples. Ironically, conservatives generally decry state involvement in the private sphere. Indeed, popular conservative arguments about social welfare are driven by the belief that family life and personal responsibility are undermined by government involvement or intervention precisely because individuals come to expect the state to resolve their family problems (Monroe, 1995). This creates a Hegelian dilemma of significant proportions. By legislating the definition, rights, and responsibilities of family in order to provide incentives for the formation of traditional families, the state actually removes the onus of family formation and maintenance from individuals and places it firmly in the public realm. This expands government's responsibility (and costs) for family maintenance rather than shrinking the size and scope of government, a key element of conservative government.

A NEW FOCUS: ALTERNATIVES TO "FAMILY" POLICY

Defining family, which is essential to creating effective family policy, is an ideological battle that is unlikely to be resolved in the near future. To create both responsible and effective family policy, policymakers should move beyond their ideological differences over the normative ideal of "family." One option is to adopt multiple definitions of family. However, specializing family policy according to the defined problems and unique needs of diverse family structures would require hundreds of definitions classified by race, ethnicity, age, economic status, etc. (Schram, 1992). In addition to being controversial, implementation of specialized policies would be impractical and costly. Indeed, abandonment of the effort to specify and limit definitions of family altogether would likely produce a much more effective and satisfactory body of family policy.

One alternative to using "family" as the unit of analysis for social policy is to gather information about and provide support to households rather than families. Households contain a number of individuals who may or may not share kinship ties (Hill, 1995). This would extend family rights and entitlements to individuals who share economic and social resources rather than extending state support based on biological ties. The household method does, however, have drawbacks. First, using households as a policy target may exclude family members who live outside of the household; for example, there would be some question as to whether fathers who have left the family would be required to transfer income to the household in which their children reside. Second, adult children and elderly parents who depend on financial transfers from their original household, but who live alone as head of the household, could be misclassified, causing legal discrepancies and policy confusion. Finally, households may contain a number of non-nuclear or unrelated individuals (unmarried couples, grandparents raising grandchildren, foster children, etc.) whose coresidency is more fluid and dynamic than that of nuclear family members. As a result, household definitions of family may overrepresent residential instability, thus making the need for government intervention or support more substantial than it really is (Rayman & Bookman, 1999).

Another alternative to family policy would take the focus off of how the state defines family and place it on where the state targets its social support. Instead of directing social assistance towards families (or households), government could choose to direct aid towards individuals or communities. The state could trace individuals from one family or household to another; this would ensure that government programs and support are portable (Hill, 1995). It would also eliminate the confusion of the definition of "family" while still allowing for family policy to meet its goal of providing for citizens' well-being. While some critics may argue that tracking individuals across households and families is impractical, the Census Bureau already collects information about individual and household mobility.

Even with any practical difficulties, the benefits of individual benefit delivery arguably outweigh the costs. If the state targeted benefits to individuals rather than determining eligibility based on family status, children who currently need health care or child care would be less likely to fall through the cracks. Rather than promoting policies that reward or penalize marriage or strictly impact single mothers, individual support for children could provide much-needed benefits like state-provided child care, afterschool care, universal school breakfast programs, etc. This idea is not entirely new, as children are the primary targets and unit of analysis for the State Children's Health Insurance Program (SCHIP), which is a subsidiary policy of Medicaid.

Finally, government could eliminate family-targeted policies in favor of programs that target whole communities. Research clearly shows that substantial benefits accrue to children who live in neighborhoods where the average income is relatively higher than the child's own family income (Brooks-Gunn, 1997; Galster, 2000; Shonkoff & Phillips, 2000; Wilson, 1987). Children who live in neighborhoods with an average median income that is at least $10,000 higher than the child's own family are 5 percent more likely to graduate from high school and 8.5 percent more likely to attend college (Tankersley, 2002). The positive effects of higher neighborhood income on relatively disadvantaged children operate via two avenues. First, disadvantaged children in relatively advantaged neighborhoods benefit from the creation of peer networks; they make connections with individuals at a higher socioeconomic status (Brooks-Gunn, 1997; Mather & Rivers, 2006; Shonkoff & Phillips, 2000; Tankersley, 2002). These networks prove important in helping the child to see beyond his own disadvantages and seek higher education. Second, having a relatively wealthy neighborhood leads to more tax revenue being pumped into social services and education (Mather & Rivers, 2006; Shonkoff & Phillips, 2000; Tankersley, 2002). Less wealthy students who would normally suffer from the lack of resources in these public institutions benefit from the contributions of their relatively advantaged neighbors.

The U.S. government has used the community policy approach with some success. The Community Development Block Grant program, created in 1974, along with the federal creation and support of

Renewal Communities, Empowerment Zones, and Enterprise Communities, provide federal funding to villages, towns, and cities for the expansion and retention of business, creation of jobs, redevelopment of abandoned buildings or lots, and provision of community centers and programs. These programs are intended to create wealth in communities, which then improves the lives and well-being of the communities' citizens and residents. Targeting such programs to entire communities eliminates any distinction between "valued" traditional, nuclear coresident families and "devalued" alternative family structures. Perhaps the community policy alternative, and the others described here, is not perceived to be politically or socially feasible or desirable in the current political environment. However, the changing nature of the American family demands a vigorous and constructive response from policymakers. Otherwise the failure of family policy is inevitable.

REFERENCES

Bramlett, M. & Mosher, W. (2001). First marriage dissolution, divorce, and remarriage: United States. *Advance Data Series* No. 323. U.S. Centers for Disease Control (www.cdc.gov).

Brooks-Gunn, J. (1997). *Neighborhood poverty: Context and consequences for children.* New York: Russell Sage Foundation.

Burstein, P.R., Bricher, M., & Einwoher, R.L., 1995. Policy alternatives and political change: Work, family, and gender on the congressional agenda, 1945–1990. *American Sociological Review, 60*(1): 67–83.

ChildTrends Social Science Research. (www.childtrends.org).

Eggebeen, D. J. & Lichter, D., (1991). Race, family structure, and changing poverty among American children. *American Sociological Review, 56*(6): 801–817.

Galster, G., (2000). The impacts of supportive housing on neighborhoods and neighbors. Urban Institute Report. Washington DC: U.S. Department of Housing and Urban Development.

Hill, M. (1995). When is a family a family? Evidence from survey data and implications for family policy. *Journal of Family and Economic Issues, 16*(1): 35–64.

Mather, M. & Rivers, K., (2006). The concentration of negative child outcomes in low-income neighborhoods. Annie E. Casey Foundation Population Reference Bureau (www.prb.org/pdf06/NegChildOutcomes_Neighborhoods.pdf).

Monroe, P., (1995). Family policy advocacy: Putting knowledge to work. *Family Relations, 44*(4): 425–437.

Murray, C., (1984). *Losing ground: American social policy, 1950–1980.* New York: Basic Books.

Oliker, S., (1994). Does workfare work? Evaluation research and workfare policy. *Social Problems, 41*(2): 195–213.

Pearce, D. (1978). The feminization of poverty: Women, work, and welfare, *Urban and Social Change Review, 30.*

Piven, F. F. & Cloward, R., (1987). The contemporary relief debate. In F. Block (Ed.), *The mean season: The attack on the welfare state.* New York: Pantheon Books.

Rayman, P. & Bookman, A., (1999). Creating a research and public policy agenda for work, family, and community. *The Evolving World of Work and Family: New Stakeholders, New Voices.* Annals of the American Academy of Political and Social Science.

Sapiro, V., (1990). The gender basis of American social policy. In L. Gordon (Ed.). *Women, the state, and welfare.* Madison: University of Wisconsin Press.

Schram, S., (1992). Post-positivistic policy analysis & the Family Support Act of 1988: Symbols at the expense of substance. *Polity, 24*(4): 633–655.

Shonkoff, J. P. & Phillips, D., (2000). *From neurons to neighborhoods: The science of early childhood development.* Washington, DC: National Academy Press.

Smith, D. S., (1993). The curious history of theorizing about the history of the western nuclear family. *Social Science History, 17*(3) 325–33.

Tankersley, H., (2002). Who are the people in your neighborhood? Measuring the effects of relative affluence on educational attainment. Catalogued Master's thesis. Washington, DC: Georgetown University. (www.georgetown.edu/library).

United States Bureau of the Census. (2007). *Family and household.* Statistics. (www.census.gov).

United States House of Representatives. (2007). *Historical legislation information.* (http://clerk.house.gov/legislative/legvotes.html).

United States Senate. (2007). *Legislation and records.* (http://www.senate.gov/pagelayout/legislative/g_three_sections_with_teasers/legislative_home.htm).

Wilson, W. J., (1987). *The truly disadvantaged: The inner city, the underclass, and public policy.* Chicago: University of Chicago Press.

Chapter 3

FAMILY VALUES, FEMINISM, AND THE POST-TRADITIONAL FAMILY

Maria K. Bachman

In *Risk Society: Towards a New Modernity* (1992), sociologist Ulrich Beck argues that modernization leads to the individual's "disembedding" or "*removal*" from historically prescribed social forms and commitments in the sense of traditional contexts of dominance and support (the 'liberating dimension'), and also leads to "the *loss of traditional security* with respect to practical knowledge, faith and guiding norms (the 'disenchantment dimension')" (p. 128). For Anthony Giddens (1994), who would agree with Beck's description, modern society is thus "post-traditional," but not in the way we might at first expect. Although we are "in a period of evident transition," one in which social life has become increasingly hectic, fractured, and uncertain, for "most of its history, modernity has rebuilt tradition as it has dissolved it," and the family, especially, is one social institution that was left largely untouched by the "radicalizing Enlightenment" (Giddens, 1994, p. 56). Tradition "is an orientation to the past, such that the past has a heavy influence or, more accurately put, is made to have a heavy influence, over the present," yet at the same time, tradition "is also about the future, since established practices are used as a way of organizing future time" (Giddens, 1994, p. 62). Tradition, therefore, is always bound up with collective memory and with the ways in which different societies presume that certain beliefs and practices and forms, such as the family, possess an "integrity and continuity which resists the buffeting of change" (Giddens, 1994, pp. 62-63). Ultimately, tradition "is an organizing medium of collective memory," and its integrity "derives not from the simple fact of persistence over time but from the continuous 'work' of interpretation that is carried out to identify the strands which bind present to past" (Giddens, 1994, p. 64).

Over the past twenty years, the structure of the American family has undergone profound and sweeping changes. There has been a marked shift away from the traditional nuclear structure, made up of two married parents—a breadwinner father and a homemaker mother—and dependent, biological children, toward an unprecedented variety of nontraditional familial arrangements, including single parents, blended and stepfamilies, gay and lesbian families, multigenerational and extended families, among others. But while the so-called "traditional" form of the American family has changed, its continuing presence as a vital social institution has not changed, and the longstanding and continuing heated debates over its "value" and its "normative" or "moral" nature only underscore that fact. This chapter offers a survey of the changing demographic realities surrounding the twenty-first century American family; discusses briefly the implications of the ongoing debates over "family values" in response to the increasing diversity of family forms; and finally, considers how feminism can productively negotiate the ideological divide between traditional and non-traditional families.

THE AMERICAN FAMILY IN TRANSITION

Family historian Stephanie Coontz (1997) observes that "today's diversity in family forms, parenting arrangements, and sex roles constitutes a tremendous sea change in family relations" (p. 108). Though the two married parents-with-children model may have been the norm a generation ago, by the year 2000, that type of family could be found in only one in four households. Despite overall increases in both the number of households and the number of people in the United States since 1990, the number of traditional families continues to drop.[1] U.S.

---

1. Between 1990 and 2000 the number of households (defined as "a person or group of people who occupy a housing unit") in the United States grew by over 13 million since 1990 (US Census 2000). "Family" households—married-couple households containing at least one person related to the householder by birth, marriage, or adoption—increased 11 percent, from 64.5 million in 1990 to 71.8 million in 2000, while "nonfamily" households—households consisting of a person living alone or a householder who shares the home with nonrelatives such as with roomates or an unmarried partner—increased by a much more dramatic 23 percent, from 27.4 million in 1990 to 33.7 million in 2000.

Census statistics show that the proportion of these families fell from 40 percent of all households in 1970 to 24 percent in 2000 and this is a trend that is likely to continue. Overall, the U.S. Census Bureau has chronicled a considerable decline in family households—two or more persons related by birth, marriage, or adoption and residing together—from 81 percent to 68 percent between 1970 and 2003. At the same time, there has been a significant increase in the number of nontraditional families over the past 40 years in America, not to mention the growing number of people who are choosing to live alone or with partners, friends, coworkers, etc., in what demographers refer to as "nonfamily" households. Childbearing outside of marriage, divorce and remarriage, cohabitation and delayed marriage, same-sex partners, and an aging population are just some of the factors that have contributed to the diversity of family forms in the United States today.

Single and Divorced Parents

The dramatic increase in single-parent families, especially those headed by women, is arguably the most significant change in the American family structure over the past fifty years. Today, more than a quarter of America's children live with one parent[2] and, according to the U.S. Bureau of Labor Statistics, more than 50 percent of all single parents with children under the age of six work outside the home.[3] Single-mother families increased from 3 million in 1970 to 10 million in 2003, while the number of single-father families grew from less than half a million to 2 million. Though many single-parent families are created as a result of unwed motherhood—the Centers for Disease Control reported that nearly four in ten U.S. babies were born outside of marriage in 2005 alone—far more result from divorce (Elliott & Umberson, 2004, p. 41).[4] Of the twelve million single-parent family groups, those with women as the primary caregivers were more likely than those maintained by men to include more than one child (45 percent compared with 37 percent). Nationally, however, there were more than

2. According to the 2000 US Census, single parents—the majority of whom are women—accounted for 27 percent of all family households with children under 18.
3. According to the US Bureau of Labor Statistics in 2005–2006, almost three out of four women with children were in the workforce.
4. More than half of all American marraiges, in fact, end in divorce. For those who then remarry, the family is reconstituted and if there are children involved, then stepparents, stepchildren, and stepsiblings are brought into the frame.

three times as many married-couple households with children as female single-parent households with children[5] and all fifty states had at least twice as many married-couple households with children as female single-parent households. Nevertheless, the Children's Defense Fund (2004) reports that one in two children will live in a single-parent family at some point in their childhood, while one in three children is born to unmarried parents.

Cohabitation/Unmarried and Same-Sex Partners

Further evidence of changing family lifestyles can be found in recent data on cohabitation. Cohabitation is defined as a family formed outside of marriage by co-residence (Elliott & Umberson, 2004, p. 36). In just one decade, the number of unmarried partner households increased by 72 percent, from three million to more than five million (U.S. Census, 2000).[6] The majority of these unmarried-partner households had partners of the opposite sex (4.9 million), but about 1 in 9 (594,000) cohabiting couples are gay and lesbian. Forty-one percent of cohabiting family households in 2000 included children under the age of 18 (compared to 46 percent of married couple households) with at least one son or daughter living in the household. Details from the 2000 U.S. Census also revealed that 96 percent of all U.S. counties have at least one same-sex couple who are raising children under the age of 18.

Multigenerational/Extended Families

Another significant shift in American family life in recent decades has been the growth—what is referred to as the "verticalization"—of the intergenerational household, family households consisting of more than two generations, such as a householder living with his or her children and grandchildren. In 2000, 64 percent of Americans over 65 lived with one or more related family members and according to a recent Harris poll survey, "The Changing Shape of the American

---

5. Although, Teachman, Tedrow and Crowder (2000) point out that the percentage of children residing with two parents, whether biological, adopted, or step, varies rather significantly by race. In 1998, 74 percent of white children, 64 percent of Hispanic children, and 36 percent of African American children lived with a mother and a father.

6. Overall, however, the majority (52 percent) of *all* households in the US were still maintained by married couples (54.5 million).

Family" (2006), nearly one in five U.S. adults with at least one child in the household also have one nonimmediate family member living there (such as an aunt, uncle, or grandparent). Moreover, the 2000 US Census reports that of the 3.9 million multigenerational households, many were likely to reside in areas where new immigrants live with their relatives, in areas where housing shortages or high costs force families to double up their living arrangements, or in areas that have relatively high rates of out-of-wedlock childbearing. At the same time, the burdens of the multigenerational family—the difficulty of balancing the competing demands of childrearing, elder care, and work—fell primarily on middle-aged female caregivers (Elliott & Umberson, 2004, p. 43).

Guardians/Foster Care

The number of children in foster care who are being cared for by members of their extended family—grandparents, aunts, uncles—also continues to increase. The Children's Defense Fund reports that one child out of 25 lives with neither parent and over half a million children were in foster care in 1999 with well over 100,000 of these children waiting for permanent adoptive families. Moreover, the 2000 U.S. Census found that approximately 6 percent of all children (4.1 million) are living in households with one or both of their grandparents.

THE 21ST CENTURY POST-TRADITIONAL FAMILY

What clearly emerges from these demographic trends is that "the traditional nuclear family is rapidly becoming an American anachronism" (*Harvard Law Review*, 1991, p. 1640)[7] and "domestic arrangements that do not conform to the traditional family unit are on the rise" (Fineman, 1995, p. 2188). Moreover, these statistics challenge the

---

7. Fineman notes that even in those families that do conform to the traditional model—married couples with children—economic survival has necessitated a shift in traditional roles. The need for a second income to keep up with the rising cost of living as well as expanded labor market opportunities has compelled women to enter the workforce, thus transforming the nuclear family into the dual-earner family: "Many women work outside the home either in a full- or part-time capacity, and some are as deeply committed to career and job advancement as their husbands" (p. 2189). According to the US Labor Bureau statistics, in 2005–2006 over two-thirds of all mothers in married-couple families were employed.

notion that "legitimate families" can only be defined through traditional, heterosexual marriage. As Fineman (1995) points out, "[f]amily affiliations are expressed in different kinds of affiliation acts":

> Some are sexually based, as with marriage. Some are forged biologically, as through parenthood. Others are more relational, such as those based on nurturing or caretaking or those developed through affection and acceptance of interdependence. (p. 2191)

Indeed, the twenty-first-century American family may be best described as post-traditional in that it does not adhere to one specific structural model: it is fluid, not static; inclusive, not exclusive; diverse, not monolithic. Perhaps most important, 97 percent of Americans in traditional families and 88 percent in nontraditional families report that they are satisfied with their family life.[8]

Despite the pluralization of forms of family life, "the social recognition and support of diverse family structures remains highly contested" (Elliott & Umberson, 2004, p. 34). As changes in the structure of the American family became more visible in the 1980s, fundamentalist Christians and conservative Republicans framed this shift in familial arrangements as a national decline in morality. Stacey (1996) notes that, while this shift was not necessarily limited to the United States, in no other society in the postindustrialized world did "the decline incite responses so volatile, ideological, divisive, or so politically mobilized and influential as in the US" (p. 87). The "family values" campaign[9] blamed the "breakdown" of the nuclear family for a staggering array of social ills ranging from poverty and teen pregnancy to low educational standards and violent crime; it also galvanized public opinion around the idea that the idealized two-parent, heterosexual family "was the panacea for all social ills in contemporary policy discussions" (Fineman, 1995, p. 2195). Moreover, there was never really any consensus as to which *values* were important, only that the traditional nuclear family–heterosexual, child-oriented, and sanctioned by marriage–was naturally (and best) suited to reproduce and transmit proper norms of social behavior to all its members. Ironically, those cru-

---

8. See *Religion & Ethics Newsweekly* poll.
9. The phrase "family values" gained considerable currency in 1992, when then-vice president Dan Quayle blasted fictional TV character Murphy Brown for having an illegitimate child. And though "family values" were central to a 2004 election drive to put same-sex marriage bans on state ballots and draw conservatives to the polls, "family values" has lost considerable ground as a key campaign issue in the 2008 election (Lawrence, 2007).

saders who were most vocal for a nostalgic return to the *Father Knows Best* world they had supposedly lost[10] were those who "contributed actively to such postmodern family statistics as divorce, remarriage, blended families, single parenthood, joint custody, abortion, domestic partnership, [and] two-career households" (Stacey, 1996, p. 87). "Family values" continues to be associated with a range of conservative causes, including opposition to the Equal Rights Amendment, single-motherhood, women working outside the home, divorce, birth control and abortion, same-sex marriage, and embryonic stem-cell research.

Sociologists and historians have pointed out, however, that the socalled (and ongoing) "family crisis"–the instability and diversification of the American family–has not been caused by the abandonment of traditional values, but by the necessity for families, however configured, to adapt to a variety of new economic and social conditions. Coontz (1992) argues that to blame the changes in family forms and values for America's social problems is a gross oversimplification. The diversity of family types emerged from "a more complicated train of events connected to the economic and political restructuring that began in the late 1960s: the eclipse of traditional employment centers, destruction of formerly high-paid union jobs, expansion of the female and minority work force, and the mounting dilemmas of welfare capitalism." Consequently, "[f]amily values, forms, and strategies that once coordinated personal life with older relations of production and distribution are now out of sync with economic and political trends" (p. 257). In her follow-up study, *The Way We Really Are* (1997), Coontz further argues that while some politicians would like to divert our attention to the plague of divorced parents and unmarried mothers, the real blame for the so-called "crisis of the family" is found in the economy, the labor market, and inadequate government policies. Dramatic domestic upheaval, in other words, has been unequivocally caused by "the historical rise in the private costs of rearing children . . . combined with the [diminishing] economic and social resources available to children of all families" (p. 145).

---

10. *Father Knows Best* was a popular American television sitcom during the late 1950s that celebrated the "ideal" middle-class family.

DIVERSIFICATION OR FRAGMENTATION?

Despite the fact that the twenty-first-century American family is not one type, but a multiplicity of types, those family forms that do not fit the normative model are consistently subject to institutional invalidation. As divorce, cohabitation, and nontraditional family situations become more widespread, the anachronistic nuclear family remains the norm against which all families are often judged and by which public policy is formed. As Johnson (2004) points out, "[i]n a society in which few people live in a nuclear family structure, the law persists in preferring and privileging this type of family" (p. 130). Johnson explains that current family laws operate under three basic assumptions: first, that "people can become Family only by birth and marriage"; second, that "Parents are people who come in pairs, [and are] preferably married"; and third, "Marriage is available only for two heterosexual individuals" (p. 126). The result of this legal bias has been a denial of social and legal benefits to individuals whose familial relationships are not defined through the ties of blood, adoption, or heterosexual marriage (*Harvard Law Review*, 1991, p. 1643). Thus, "the law's current preference for a certain family structure harms both those who do and do not take that form" (Johnson, 2004, p. 130). In fact, heterosexual married couples and their families receive a plethora of legal protections and benefits in state and federal law that are not available to other committed domestic partners, including social security, Medicare, family leave, health care, disability, military benefits, and parenting rights.[11] Furthermore, many of these benefits are hidden direct and indirect subsidies through tax, inheritance, marriage, and other laws (Fineman, 1995, p. 2205). For instance, unmarried couples, whether heterosexual or homosexual, are generally not eligible for "spousal" health and life insurance benefits unless their employer provides such progressive options.

Though a recent survey on religion and the family indicates that an overwhelming majority of Americans (82 percent) are opposed to the

---

11. In 1996, then President Clinton signed into law the "Defense of Marriage Act," which restricts the ability of same-sex couples to have their relationships recognized at the state and federal levels. This law defines marriage as "only a legal union between one man and one woman as husband and wife, and the word 'spouse' refers only to a person of the opposite sex who is a husband or a wife," and prohibits same-sex couples from receiving any of the federal protections afforded married couples. This legislation has enabled states to pass laws that deny recognition of same-sex couples' civil marraiges from other states.

government's involvement in encouraging marriage, the strengthening of marriage as an institution nevertheless continues to move up the nation's social policy agenda as evidenced in several initiatives proposed by the Bush Administration and members of Congress. For example, the Healthy Marriage Initiative was launched in 2002 to promote marriage, particularly among low-income Americans, as a way of fighting poverty and reducing the number of single-parent households. The federal government has also awarded more than $25 million in pro-marriage grants for demonstration projects, including grants to 42 faith-based and community organizations nationwide to support their capacity to build and deliver programs that support marriage.

For too long, Fineman (1995) argues, "family policy in [the U.S.] has been fashioned to further the nuclear family ideal" (p. 2214), while family affiliations or arrangements that do not conform to the traditional nuclear mode–single-parent families, interracial families, gay families, among others–continue to be legally stigmatized and those individual rights and freedoms supposedly promised by a democratic society. Despite the reality of how people really live, public debate in the media and in Congress[12] continues to revolve around the definition of family and which kind of "family" is "best" for a stable, functioning society with "[l]iberals, conservatives, and progressives (including most feminists) [still] divided over marriage, women's equality, child rearing, and welfare" (Baca Zinn, 2000, p. 52). Yet, pro-family politicians frequently oppose policies that would benefit families, such as those enabling affordable access to education and healthcare, raising wages for all workers so that their families can be adequately supported, and protecting the interests of families against large corporate interests such as predatory lenders, polluters, and privatized utilities (Stacey, 1996). When politicians make bold claims to restore family values, they simultaneously devalue the material conditions of American family life.

---

12. Stacey (1996) notes that "crisis of family often incites acrimonious conflicts in every imaginable arena–from television sitcoms to Congress, from the Boy Scouts of America to the United States Marines, from local school boards to multinational corporations, from art museums to health insurance writers, from Peoria to Cairo, and from political conventions to social science conferences" (pp. 87–88).

REDEFINING FAMILY VALUES

Paradoxically, "family values" has become a euphemism for injustice and discrimination. Indeed, "[i]n a culture which holds the two-parent patriarchal family in higher esteem than any other arrangement," argues cultural critic bell hooks (2000), "all children feel emotionally insecure when their family does not measure up to the standard" (p. 77). Johnson (2004) argues that "[t]he time has come for a reconsideration of family unburdened by biases toward the two-parent heterosexual role-divided model" (p. 143). Coontz (1997) similarly challenges the myth that the maledominated nuclear family is essential for a smoothly functioning society and argues that many forms of families are effective and valuable: "[m]any of the problems commonly blamed on breakdown of the traditional family exist not because we've changed too much but because we haven't changed enough . . . it is the *lag* in adjusting values, behaviors, and institutions to new realities that creates problems in contemporary families" (p. 109). While the structure of the twenty-first century family is undeniably much changed from the traditional two-parent nuclear model, the American family, in all its diverse forms, remains vital to the health of our communities and our entire society. The real aim then of our social institutions should be to find ways to help the post-traditional family, in all its shapes and sizes, to flourish. Family values must not be a moral imaginary, but a moral reality, one that could be greatly enhanced in feminist thinking and practice.

Rethinking family values means first, acknowledging the diversity of family forms and affectional ties, particularly since both nontraditional families (49 percent) and traditional families (37 percent) are concerned that their children learn the right values (*Religion & Ethics*). Given the fact that the United States has always defined itself through a multiplicity of ethnic, religious, and cultural traditions, as Fineman argues, "we should develop a pluralistic social model inclusive of diverse family practices" (1995, p. 2189). Further, Coontz (1997) recommends that we alter our values in ways that broaden responsibility for taking care of each other and especially taking care of children. In reforming family values for the twenty-first-century family, there is much to be gleaned, according to bell hooks (2000), from feminist thinking: "Feminist thinking and practice emphasize the value of mutual growth and self-actualization in partnerships and in parenting.

[It is a] vision of relationships where everyone's needs are respected, where everyone has rights, where no one need fear subordination or abuse" (p. 77). Indeed, *feminist values* of love, mutual respect, care, responsibility, compassion, and integrity, should and can be *family values*. Though 80 percent of Americans polled believe that it is better for children if their parents are married, 55 percent agreed that "love is what makes a family" (*Religion & Ethics*). Indeed, hooks (2000) notes that "[l]oving parents, be they single or coupled, gay or straight, headed by females or males, are more likely to raise healthy, happy children with sound self-esteem" (p. 77). Family values are indeed vital to the stability of American society, but these values must reflect the reality of American society. Stacey (1996) suggests that we begin by "redefin[ing] family values democratically by extending full rights, obligations, resources, and legitimacy to a diversity of intimate bonds" (p. 77).

What families really need is not to try to achieve a 1950s ideal, but instead to alter our social context; it is time to devote our energies and resources to how the family can best function rather than what it should look like (Coontz, 1992, 1997; Johnson, 2004)). As Elliot and Umberson (2004) point out, "within any particular family form, the quality of the relationships therein determines the value or the risk of that family form for adults and children" (p. 48). Our rhetorical concern for "the family in crisis" needs to be supported with polices that commit to the value of family. Whatever their configuration, families continue to be the primary source of shelter, support, and comfort for their members, both young and old; it is the foremost site in our society for care-giving and care-receiving. As Fineman (1995) reminds us, "[t]he ideology of the private family mandates that the unit nurture its members and provide for them economically" (p. 2187). Family life, however, has become much more difficult in recent decades due to cutbacks in social support systems, economic decline for working families, and growing poverty for the unemployed or marginally employed (Coontz, 1997, p. 145). These economic and social trends have weakened this vital support structure, making it more difficult for too many families to provide nurturance and vital support to children, spouses, partners, aging relatives, etc.

With over 50 percent of American children living in a family that does not fit the traditional model, it is unproductive to continue debating the relative merits of the "perfect" family types. "The time has come," Johnson (2004) argues, "for a reconsideration of family unburdened by biases toward the two-parent heterosexual role-divided model" (p. 143). According to Fineman (1995), "we must begin to rethink the institution of the contemporary family in a way that is responsive to emerging realities" (p. 2203). We must, in other words, reinvest in all families. Families, of all shapes and sizes, will be strengthened only when they are all regarded as "legitimate" and when their economic stability is taken seriously by policy makers. Coontz (1992) argues that the ongoing debate around families has been mistakenly posed as one of values versus the economy when, in fact, those two factors are interdependent. If we want to become a society that truly values family, then we must promote public policies and necessary changes in our economy that address the needs of all families. Real democratic family values provide affordable, quality childcare programs for working parents; access to healthcare for parents, children, and elders; access to affordable family housing; paid family and medical leave for all workers;[13] fair pay and benefits for part-time employees; and more flexible work schedules, among other family-friendly work policies.

FEMINIST FAMILY VALUES

Equality, mutual respect, and justice have always been at the forefront of feminist thinking and practice, and yet, feminism has long been misunderstood as antifamily. In reality, feminism has always aimed at inclusiveness, not divisiveness. In challenging an "ideal" institution that thwarted equal participation and mutual respect in the private sphere, feminists have been accused of being antifamily. In their tireless advocacy of reproductive freedom, family and medical leave, pay equity, and child care, feminists have actually been pro-family all along. It is time to realize, as hooks (2000) tells us, that feminism is, indeed, for everybody. Coontz (1992) argues that the so-called "crisis of the family" is a "subset of a much larger crisis of social

---

13. While the Family and Medical Leave Act (signed into law in 1993) acknowledges the difficult choices that almost every family in America faces regarding job and parenting responsibilities, and has thus established a sound precedent in federal family care policy, the U.S. still does not guarantee paid leave for parents in any segment of the workforce. (FMLA provides up to twelve weeks of unpaid leave for the birth of a child or the onset of a serious illness.)

obligation that requires us to look beyond private family relations and rebuild larger social ties" (p. 283). She recommends that we alter our values in ways that broaden responsibility for taking care of each other and especially taking care of children:

> To handle social obligations and interdependency in the twenty-first century, we must abandon any illusion that we can or should revive some largely mythical traditional family. We need to invent new family traditions and find ways of reviving older community ones, not wallow in nostalgia for the past or heap contempt on people whose family values do not live up to ours. (pp. 277–78)

Indeed, we can no longer claim to live in a just and equitable society as long as those families who do not fit the ideal model are vilified in public discourse and in public policy. We need, instead, a "reformulated vision of justice" that recognizes "the claim of [all] caretakers for [cultural and economic] resources necessary to accomplish their nurturing tasks" (Fineman, 1995, p. 2214). We must reassess the American family in terms of a progressive partnership, a "humane social 'contract' [that is] based on the spirit of collective responsibility and an appreciation of the generalized interdependence among all members of society" (Fineman, 1995, p. 2194).

REFERENCES

Baca Zinn, M. (2000). Feminism and family studies for a new century. *Annals of the American Academy of Political and Social Science, 571*, 42–56.

Beck, U. (1992). *Risk society: Towards a new modernity.* Trans. Mark Ritter. London: SAGE Publications.

Children's Defense Fund. (2004). *The state of America's children.* Washington, DC.

Coontz, S. (1992). *The way we never were. American families and the nostalgia trap.* New York: Basic Books.

Coontz, S. (1997). *The way we really are: Coming to terms with America's changing families.* New York: Basic Books.

Elliott, S., & Umberson, D. (2004). Recent demographic trends in the US and implications for well-being. In J. Scott, J. Treas, & M. Richards (Eds.), *The Blackwell companion to the sociology of families* (pp. 17–33). Oxford: Blackwell.

Fineman, M. (1995). Masking dependency: The political role of family rhetoric. *Virginia Law Review, 81*(8), 2181–2215.

Giddens, A. (1994). Living in a post-traditional society. In U. Beck, A. Giddens, & S. Lash (Eds.), *Reflexive modernization: Politics, tradition, and aesthetics in the modern social order* (pp. 56–109). Cambridge: Polity Press.

Harris Interactive. (2006). Survey: The Changing Shape of the American Family. Retrieved on July 21, 2007, from http://research.lawyers.com/The-Changing-Shape-of-the-American-Family.html.

hooks, b. (2000). *Feminism is for everybody*. Cambridge, MA: South End Press.

Johnson, J. R. (2004). Preferred by law: The disappearance of the traditional family and law's refusal to let it go. *Women's Rights Law Reporter, 25* (2–3), 125–144.

Lawrence, J. (2007, December 17). 'Family values' lower on agenda in 2008 race. USA Today. Retrieved April 1, 2008, from http://www.usatoday.com/news/politics/election2008/2007-12-17Familyvalues_N.htm.

Note. (1991). Looking for a family resemblance: The limits of the functional approach to the legal definition of family. *Harvard Law Review, 104*(7), 1640–1659.

Religion & Ethics Newsweekly. (2005). Survey: Faith and family in America. Retrieved on July 21, 2007, from http://www.pbs.org/net/religionandethics/week908/survey.html.

Stacey, J. (1996). *In the name of the family: Rethinking family values in the postmodern age*. Boston: Beacon Press.

Teachman, J., Tedrow, L., & Crowder, K. (2000). The changing demography of America's families. *Journal of Marriage and the Family, 62*, 1234–1246.

U.S. Bureau of the Census. (2001). Households and families. *Census 2000 Brief.* Washington, DC: US Government Printing Office.

U.S. Bureau of the Census. (2003). Married-couple and unmarried-couple households. *Census 2000 Special Report.* Washington, DC: US Government Printing Office.

U.S. Bureau of the Census. (2004). America's families and living arrangements: Population characteristics 2003. *Current Population Reports, Series* P20-553.Washington, DC: US Government Printing Office.

U.S. Bureau of Labor Statistics. (2007). Employment Characteristics of Families. Table 5: Employment status of the population by sex, marital status, and presence and age of own children under 18, 2005-06 annual averages. Retrieved on July 16, 2007, from http://www.bls.gov/news.release/famee.t05.htm.

U.S. Bureau of Labor Statistics. (2007). Employment Characteristics of Families. Table 6. Employment status of mothers with own children under 3 years old by single year of age of youngest child and marital status, 2005-06 annual averages. Retrieved on July 16, 2007, http://www.bls.gov/news.release/famee.t06.htm.

U.S. Bureau of Labor Statistics. (2004). Employment Characteristics of Families Summary, 2006. Retrieved on July 16, 2007, from http://www.bls.gov/news.release/famee.nr0.htm.

Chapter 4

THE MANY FACES OF ADOPTION IN THE TRANSFORMATION OF THE AMERICAN FAMILY

Patricia S. Piver

Adoption*: The process of choosing to bring into a relationship, as into one's own family.*

The first settlers on the American continent defined family as a social unit consisting of father, mother, and children. Since the first colonies were established by European explorers in the 1600s, the traditional family has evolved into the concept of two or more people who usually live in the same dwelling and share common values, goals, and commitments (Family, n.d.). The family is still considered the foundation of society although the makeup of family has changed significantly over the years. Adoption has become the most common path taken by those choosing to create a family through nontraditional, legal means.

ADOPTION: PAST TO PRESENT

Adoption has always existed with roots that can be traced to the Code of Hammurabi and Hindu Sanskrit texts. Early practices took place when children were abandoned or parents died and family members took children into their homes. Many ancient civilizations such as China and Rome witnessed infertile couples and parents who did not have sons adopt males who were to become heirs, carry on the family name, and participate in religious ceremonies (Pertman, 2000). English history records informal placement of illegitimate or orphaned children long before the twentieth century. These practices were brought to the American colonies where they were adapted to meet the needs of colonial society. The southern plantation system, for example, included the informal transfer of dependent children for farm labor. Other common practices included adoption petitions, charitable adoptions, informal adoptions, and indenture. None of these included formal, legal adoptions that are prevalent today.

In the 1700s, adoption petitions were sought to ensure legal recognition of a child's changed status and right of inheritance (Cahn & Hollinger, 2004). Adoption petitions were made to state legislatures and are documented in Louisiana, Texas, Vermont, and Massachusetts between 1781 and the end of the Civil War in 1865. Charitable adoptions came about as a result of the massive influx of immigrants and the hardships of the Industrial Revolution in the 1800s. Poor housing, unclean water, lack of adequate sewage, and harsh working conditions led to high death rates resulting in orphans and homeless children left to wander the streets of major cities. Organizations, usually associated with religious movements, tried to find permanent homes for unwanted children. Some organizations, such as the American Female Moral Reform and Guardian Society of New York, sought to place children through adoption or service (apprenticeship) (Ibid.). In spite of the efforts of many charitable agencies, the number of children without parents rose.

Informal adoptions occurred when parents willingly allowed their children to be raised by another person, usually a relative. This system of adoption was widely practiced by African-American families following the end of slavery at the end of the Civil War in 1865 (Pertman, 2000). Informal adoptions also included deeding children to adoptive parents by biological parents. The practice treated children as chattel and continued until the twentieth century.

The practice of indenture met the needs of a growing society through providing hired help or apprentices within the same social class. Indenture contracts placed children in foster homes allowing for shared custody with parents who received compensation (Cahn & Hollinger, 2004). Through this practice many children were completely alienated from their biological parents.

The Massachusetts Act of 1851 was the first American adoption law setting the precedent for court approval of new parents for children. It is credited as the first adoption statute to focus on the interests of children and the beginning point for modern adoption law (Ibid.). The law was passed in response to the inability of the public child welfare system to handle the tens of thousands of children left to wander the streets during the mid-1800s. It marked the origin of mandatory court approval for adoptions by the states.

Following the Massachusetts Act of 1851, private and public "foundling homes" appeared attempting to aid the orphans of the streets (Pertman, 2000). Good intentions aimed at alleviating the problem became warehouses of disease and did not help and, potentially, worsened the situation. The orphan train movement, begun by Reverend Charles Loring Brace in New York, transported as many as 100,000 children from eastern cities to farms in the western states. Biological parents unable to provide for their children suffered heartbreak and loss.

The early years of the twentieth century in America were marked by a movement toward secrecy in which state statutes, such as the Minnesota Act of 1917, sealed adoption records (Cahn & Hollinger, 2004). The "secrecy" movement was twofold. First, single, pregnant women were shamed into entering homes for unwed mothers. They were given fictitious names, wedding bands to wear in public, and encouraged not to ruin their lives by raising an illegitimate child. They disappeared from their homes and families until after the child was born and given up for adoption. Second, adoptive parents were physically matched to illegitimate babies and new birth certificates were prepared with the adoptive parents listed as birth parents. Sealed adoptions were designed to protect the adoptive parents from feelings of inadequacy and embarrassment. Adopted children were shielded from labels such as bastard, and, many times, were never told that they were adopted. Records were sealed and marked, "illegitimate" (Pertman, 2000). The closed adoption movement is still enforced today in many states.

Adoption practices became more visible during the 1950s when Korean war orphans were brought to the United States. Many of them were biracial having both Korean and American heritage. Adoptive parents began to acknowledge that their children were adopted and searches for birth parents or personal information were not attempted.

Between 1948 and 1953, war orphans from Germany, Greece, other European nations, and Asian children from Japan were adopted by childless couples in America (Ibid.). As these countries rebuilt their economies, however, they closed the doors to foreign adoption requests. Following the Vietnam War of the 1970s, Vietnamese and other Southeast Asian orphans were brought to the United States. These light skinned, young children were more easily woven into the American traditional family unit, especially if they were fathered by American soldiers.

The cultural revolutions of the 1970s and 1980s brought changes in attitudes toward single parenting and relaxed the moral stigma of raising children born out of wedlock by birth parents (Ibid.). Today's nontraditional family is represented by single parents, divorced parents, stepparents, parents of one gender, children born through sperm or egg donation, surrogate mothers, and interracial marriage. Most Americans consider the nontraditional parenting normal rather than abnormal. Transracial adoption, particularly between Caucasian and African-American races, has raised controversy and is still a hotly debated issue focused on preserving cultural heritage (Patton, 2000). Other concerns include nontraditional parenting through open adoptions.

The secrecy of early adoptions has evolved into the open adoptions practiced today. During the 1950s, the number of available infants equaled that of couples seeking to adopt (Pertman, 2000). Today, there are six couples for every white baby available to be adopted. The impact of the availability of contraceptives and number of unwed mothers raising their babies has heightened the search for infants including a willingness to consider the open adoption option. In an open adoption, the birth mother and adoptive parents enter into a relationship that is sustained after the placement of the child. The benefits for adoptive parents include easing personal insecurities and a steady stream of information including medical history. Benefits for the birth mother include diminished fear and higher comfort levels. While each situation can differ, the adoptive parents usually set the parameters for visits and contact with the child. No system is perfect and open adoption has its pitfalls (Ibid.). It is unusual for adoptees to seek their birth parents until they reach their twenties. Open adoption has become a strong component in the transformation of the American family.

THE CHANGING FACES OF ADOPTIVE PARENTS

The traditional family and the extended family of grandparents, great-grandparents, and other relatives formed a support group for children during the early years of American history. The current divorce rate of 50 percent, legalized gay marriage, interracial marriage, and modern scientific technology in the field of fertilization have merged to create a new concept of family (Ibid.).

Single, gay, and lesbian adoptive parents can be found throughout the population of the United States. Co-parent adoption allows a secure, legal relationship with a child, and, in many situations, one partner in a same-sex relationship will adopt a partner's biological or adopted child to ensure that there are two legal parents to provide for and support the child. Often, a single will adopt a special needs child and later add the partner as the child's second parent, similar to adoption by a stepparent (Cahn & Hollinger, 2004). The state of Florida is the only state at present that bars gay adoptions. Other states do not bar gay adoptions, but do not practice them. Alabama, Georgia, Kentucky, Tennessee, Ohio, and Missouri are currently considering constitutional amendments or laws to ban gay adoption. In 1998, the U.S. Census Bureau reported that there were 170,000 same-sex couples having a child living in the home. It is estimated that the numbers have grown exponentially in the last ten years. The controversy of gay, lesbian, and single parents has spawned research to determine if there are possible negative outcomes of the practices. Data analysis shows no significant differences (U.S. Department of Health and Human Services, 2000).

Middle-aged, divorced, widowed, and childless singles struggle to adopt under scrutiny of homosexuality. In the American culture, men tend to face more intense scrutiny to adopt since women typically are considered to be more nurturing and are more likely to raise children alone. Once the single has been determined to be "safe," the process can take years to complete (Pertman, 2000). For the middle-aged prospective parents, time is crucial since most states prefer younger parents.

The Multiethnic Placement Act of 1994, passed by both houses of Congress, paved the way for transracial/transcultural adoptions (Patton, 2000). Estimates suggest that as many as 1,000 to 2,000 African-American children in the United States are adopted by white families each year in addition to the children adopted from other countries. The shortage of white babies and cost of international adoptions have led to a rise in transracial adoptions through public adoption services. The practice is widely debated in society but not barred in any state. Opponents stress the need to preserve and strengthen the culture and history of the racial/ethnic group while supporters promote "color-blindness" and focus on the best interest of the child (Ibid.). The human drive to share in the fulfilling experience of raising children impacts society's acceptance of parents considered nontraditional.

CURRENT TRENDS IN ADOPTION – FACTS AND FIGURES

The current population of the United States is 301,840,756 (U.S. Census Bureau, 2007). Approximately 130,000 to 150,000 adoptions are approved by United States' courts each year, including babies and young children, in 30,000 to 40,000 of the total adoptions approved. Data suggests that over 21,000 babies and young children are adopted from foreign countries today, an increase over the estimated 6,500 in 1992 (Child Welfare Information Gateway, 2004). The Evan B. Donaldson Adoption Institute conducted a survey in 1997 and documented that six in ten Americans have had personal experience with adoption in some form (Evan B. Donaldson Adoption Institute, 1997). It is clear that adoption has become a common legal practice among U.S. citizens.

Several forms of adoption are practiced today including public, private, kinship, stepparent, transracial, and intercountry/international (Cahn & Hollinger, 2004). Public adoptions involve the placement of children in permanent homes by government-operated agencies or private agencies under contract with the government to place children. Children waiting for adoption in foster homes make up a majority of public adoptions. Requests for babies have been discouraged due to the availability of abortion, contraceptives, and the choice of unmarried mothers to keep their infants. Most children in foster homes are young children and teens. There are an estimated 532,000 children in foster care with 129,000 of them available for adoption (National Adoption Information Clearinghouse, 2000a). The cost for public adoptions is less than both private and international adoptions. Public adoptions account for approximately 16 percent of all adoptions. In contrast, private adoptions involve placement of children in nonrelative homes by nonprofit, or for-profit, agencies sometimes licensed by the state. Private adoptions account for approximately 40 percent of total adoptions and are more costly than public adoptions (Ibid.).

Kinship and stepparent adoptions combine to make up approximately 42 percent of the current adoptions in America. Kinship adoptions occur as a result of the death, abuse, or termination of parental rights. In some circumstances, siblings become adoptive parents. Transracial adoptions are when children are placed with an adoptive parent/family of another race. The 8 percent estimate of transracial adoptions includes intercountry/international adoptions (Child Welfare Information Gateway, 1994; Transracial Adoption, 2007).

The United States Department of Agriculture estimates the cost of adoption to be between $15,000 and $30,000 depending on the type of adoption chosen (The Costs of Adopting, 2007). All forms of adoption include the cost of a home study and court costs. Other expenses that may occur are agency fees, post placement supervision, parent physicals, psychiatric examinations, advertising, document preparation, and petition and court representation for finalization. If the adoption is an open adoption and birth parents are involved, medical expenses and living expenses are added to the total. Sometimes counseling and legal representation for the birth parents are also necessary. If an intercountry/international adoption is undertaken, costs may vary, but usually include donations to the foreign orphanage involved, translators, travel, foreign court representation, state department fees (filing, immigrant visa application/issuance), agency fees, U.S. agency representative, and medical or psychological evaluations (Ibid.). It is easy to see how some foreign adoptions may exceed the $30,000 figure. The wealthy set a high standard and median income Americans generally cannot compete. The United States Census notes that the median income of adoptive families is $56,000 and adoptive parents tend to be older than parents who have biological children. More adoptive parents have bachelor's degrees and own their own homes than younger, biological parents (Adoption EDU, 2007). The financial concerns of those involved in adopting an infant often limit middle class members' and lower class persons' abilities to create the nontraditional family through adoption.

THE RISE IN POPULARITY OF ADOPTION

Modern technology has played a major role in the rise in popularity of adoption. Public disclosure of the lives of movie stars, politicians, and the rich and famous reveals a new phenomenon in adoption. The Hollywood adoption craze has focused attention on both single parenting and foreign sources for children (Families.com Forums, 2006). Hollywood has had a long history of adoption although disclosure has been a recent change. Julie Andrews and her second husband adopted two Vietnamese girls in 1974 at a time when few prominent stars raised non-European children. Other actors and actresses followed her lead with recent adoptive parents receiving international attention. Angelina Jolie became a single parent of children from Cambodia (2002), Ethiopia (2005), and Vietnam (2007). Meg Ryan adopted a child from China in 2006. Madonna, considered the Queen of Pop, stirred international controversy when she adopted a young boy from Malawi whose father placed him in an orphanage following the death of his mother from AIDS. She agreed to bring the boy for a visit and to encourage knowledge of traditions and customs of his people (Recent Trends in International Adoption, 2003). Human rights groups criticize Hollywood adoptions citing the advantage of the wealthy and famous to "cherry-pick" children from the Third World, but public sentiment is favorable.

Nearly half of the foreign adopted children come from China and Russia. Recently, Russia imposed restrictions on adoptive parents which has heightened interest in other countries still open to foreign adoptions. In 2005, the U.S. Department of State listed the following top twenty countries from which Americans adopted children.

1. China
2. Russia
3. Guatemala
4. South Korea
5. Ukraine
6. Kazakhstan
7. India
8. Vietnam
9. Colombia
10. Haiti
11. Philippines
12. Romania
13. Bulgaria
14. Belarus
15. Ethiopia
16. Cambodia
17. Poland
18. Thailand
19. Azerbaijan
20. Mexico

(Ibid.). Media coverage of foreign adoptions has heightened the interest in transracial and intercountry/international adoptions.

The Internet has made it much easier to locate current information on adoption agencies, adoption lawyers, state laws governing requirements of adoptive parents, the adoption process, and adoption packets. Individuals can even view photographs and biographical descriptions of available children both in America and many foreign countries. Advertisements seeking surrogate parents and unborn babies are common in all forms of media. The information age has brought opportunities to all members of society to explore and gain information on adoptions of all types. Correspondence between individuals all over the world has brought the process to a personal level (Pertman, 2000).

THE FACE OF ADOPTION IN EDUCATION

The transformation of American attitudes toward family structure through adoption has had an impact on other facets of the culture. For example, the revelation of the number of adoptions, both closed and open, needs to encourage the educational system to broaden the definition of diversity in the classroom (Child Welfare Information Gateway, 1993). Diversity and multicultural education are especially important topics in American educational centers. The adopted child may or may not be obvious in the school setting, but should be supported and accepted by the public school. Certain activities and statements can have a negative effect upon the adopted child's self-esteem and self-concept.

A positive school environment begins with the awareness of the diverse needs and sensitivities of adopted children by administration and staff (Child Welfare Information Gateway, 2004). Terminology associated with family issues should be adapted to include all family possibilities. Common assignments/activities that have negative effects on adopted children, such as designing family trees, should be adapted to reflect current and more relevant family structures. Opportunities to learn about diversities and how to relate to children who are different need to be provided through workshops and coursework for all faculty and staff.

It is important that curriculum and daily lessons be adapted to include multicultural and diverse family situations. Adopted children from foreign countries should have their cultures and ethnicity celebrated for their contributions throughout the year instead of emphasized only on holidays. Derogatory racial and ethnic comments must be eliminated and used as learning experiences when they do occur. The creation of a school family, including all students in a class, helps promote understanding of today's nontraditional family.

THE FACE OF ADOPTION IN THE FUTURE

Openness in adoption appears to represent the face of adoption in the future. Informal, and sometimes formal, agreements between birth parents and adoptive parents will address issues of concern and connections often will continue throughout their lives. The number of teenagers giving birth to babies available for adoption is likely to decrease according to the latest data presented by the Center for Human Statistics. The predicted decrease will continue, due in part to the United States' encouragement to do so, indicated by a bill signed by President Bill Clinton in 1996 providing billions of dollars to the states to promote sexual abstinence (Pertman, 2000).

Homosexual relationships will increasingly become a fact of life with adoption playing a critical role in the social transformation of the concept of family. States are becoming more receptive to allowing singles, gays, and lesbians to adopt children, especially children who are hard to place due to disabilities or race. Dealing with rejection has slowed the progress but will not equal the perseverance shown by singles.

The rise in adoptions in America raises questions about new technologies and scientific advancements including sperm bank donors' rights and embryo storage and transfer. The possibilities of selling embryos through the World Wide Web concern both governmental agencies and human rights activists. There are currently about 200,000 frozen embryos in laboratories in America (Ibid.). Incidents of marriage between siblings and news stories of doctors who injected their own sperm into numerous patients have resulted in filing systems similar to those used in closed adoptions. The future is riddled with ethical, medical, and legal issues that will continue the transformation of adoption in America.

CONCLUSION

The social unit known as family is experiencing a transformation from a genetically connected group to a unit voluntarily bound by values, common goals, and commitments. History has seen the shift from closed adoptions to open adoptions forming a triad between the child, birth parent and adoptive parents who work together for the benefit of the child. Statistics indicate that the majority of the legal adoptions in America are kinship adoptions followed by public, private, and international adoptions. There has been a notable rise in the interest in adoptions, especially on the international level. Recent adoptions by the rich and famous have brought transracial/international adoptions to the forefront of national news in newspapers, magazines, and the Internet. The influx of adopted children into the educational environment broadens the definition of diversity and multicultural education. Parents and social workers are working to help schools provide for the special needs of the adopted child. The future holds many new issues for the individual desiring to become a parent. Singles, gay, and lesbian citizens will become parents in increasing numbers.

The United States has grown as it has welcomed immigrants from every country of the world and adopted them into a multicultural society. The family remains the foundation for the society, but the structure of the family has evolved from traditional to nontraditional. This transformation represents a strength of the American culture.

REFERENCES

Adoption EDU. (2007). Adoption statistics. Retrieved April 20, 2007, from www.adoptionedu.com/AdoptionStatistics.htm.

Cahn, N. R., & Hollinger, J.H. (Eds.). (2004). *Families by law.* New York: New York University Press.

Child Welfare Information Gateway. (2004). *Appendix A: Total Adop-tions for 1987, 1989, 1990, 1991, 1992, 2000, and 2001.* Retrieved April 26, 2007, from www.childwelfare.gov.pubs/s_adopted/ s_adoptedf.cfm.

Child Welfare Information Gateway. (1993). *Adoption and school issues: Increasing the adoption sensitivity of school personnel.* Retrieved April 26, 2007, from www.child-welfare.gov/pubs/f_school/f_shoolf.cfm.

Child Welfare Information Gateway. (1994). *Transracial and transcultural adoption.* Retrieved April 27, 2007, from www.childwelfare.gov/ pubs/f_trans.cfm.

Clement, P.F. (1997). *Growing pains: Children in the industrial age, 1850–1890.* New York: Twayne.

Evan B. Donaldson Adoption Institute. (1997). *Benchmark adoption survey: Report on findings.* [Conducted by Princeton Survey Research Associates]. New York: Evan B. Donaldson Adoption Institute.

Evan B. Donaldson Adoption Institute. (2007). *Resource guide for educators.* Retrieved April 15, 2007, from www.adoptioninstitute.org/ proed/educators.html.

Families.com Forums. (2006). Retrieved May 15, 2007, from www. forums.families.com/another-hollywood-star-meg-ryan-adopts-baby-from-china-jan.

Family. (n.d.). Retrieved May 5, 2007, from www.answers.com/family &r=67.

General Court of Massachusetts, An Act to Provide for the Adoption of Children, *Acts and resolves passed by the general court of Massachusetts* (Boston, 1851), Chap 324, pp. 815–16.

Holt International Children's Services. (2000). *International adoption statistics: Significant source countries of immigrant orphans 1985–1996.* Retrieved April 29, 2007, from ww.holtintl.org/insstats.html.

Ladner, J.A. (1977). Mixed families: Adopting across racial boundaries. Garden City, N Y: Doubleday.

National Adoption Information Clearinghouse. (2000a). *Adoption numbers and trends.* Retrieved May 2, 2007, from www.calib.com/naic/adptsear/adoption/research/stats/numbers.html.

National Adoption Information Clearinghouse. (2000b). *Access to adoption records.* Retrieved April 26, 2007, from www.calib.com/naic/factsheets/acctxt.htm.

National Committee for Adoption. (n.d.). *Adoption factbook: United States data, issues, regulations and resources* (Washington, D.C.: National Committee for Adoption 1989).

Nelson, C. (2003). *Little strangers.* Bloomington, IN: Indiana University Press.

Patton, S. (2000). *BirthMarks.* New York: New York University Press.

Pertman, A. (2000). *Adoption nation.* New York: Basic Books.

Recent Trends in International Adoption. (2003). Retrieved on May 15, 2007, from www.adopting.org/adoptions/recent-trends-in-international-adoption.html.

Same-sex Marriage in the United States. (n.d.). Retrieved April 24, 2007, from http://en.wikipedia.org/wiki/Same-sex_marriage_in_ the_United_States.

The Costs of Adopting: A Factsheet for Families. (2007). Retrieved May 4, 2007, from www.costs.adoption.com/articles/the-costs-of-adopting-a-factsheet-for-families.html.

Transracial Adoption. (2007). *What is transracial adoption?* Retrieved April 25, 2007, from Statistids.adoption.com/information/interracial-adoption-statistics.html.

U.S. Census Bureau. (2007). *U.S. POPClock projection.* Retrieved May 2, 2007, from www.census.gov/population/www/popclockus.html.

U.S. Department of Health and Human Services, *The AFCARS report: Current estimates as of March 2000.* Retrieved April 23, 2007, Washington, D.C.: Administration for Children and Families. (1999). www.acf.dhhs.gov/programs/cb/Stats/tarreport/rpt0100/ar0100.htm.

Chapter 5

GRANDPARENTING ROLES IN THE EVOLVING AMERICAN FAMILY

William E. Hills

The status and authority of grandparents in the American family has changed considerably over the last 150 years, reflecting variations in social, economic, political, and demographic trends (Szinovacz, 1998, for a review). The shift from the extended to nuclear family form prompted by the industrial revolution resulted in fewer interactions and less influence for grandparents with family members and traditional decision-making processes (Harbert & Ginsberg, 1990). Extended family bonds based on property ownership and frequent visits disintegrated with employment driven migrations away from the farms and small towns. Nuclear family ideals of autonomy and self-sufficiency instituted for childrearing marginalized grandparents and changed the perceived value of grandparent/grandchild interactions (Vann, 2004). In the twentieth century, as the number of older adults increased with life expectancy gains, grandparents became companions for grandchildren (Kahana & Kahana, 1971; Neugarten & Weinstein, 1964). The nuclear family ideal of generational independence allowed grandparents to participate socially with grandchildren but not to interfere with parental rights regarding childrearing practices. The concept of the indulgent grandparent, who wanted neither authority nor responsibility, developed during this time (Albrecht, 1954; Apple, 1956).

There is one role of the grandparent, however, that, regardless of temporal events or social circumstances, seems to appear consistently in the literature: Grandparents have always served the family as a source of crisis support. Whether conceptualized, in the earliest studies of grandparenthood, as the "rescuer" if "the intervening generation fails" (Albrecht, 1954; cited by Szinovacz, 1998; Von Hentig, 1946), the "surrogate parent" in the seminal study of grandparenting style by Neugarten and Weinstein (1964), the "safety valve" for families in crisis (Cherlin & Furstenberg, 1986), or, most recently, as the "vital safety net" by the American Association of Retired Persons (AARP, 2006), grandparents have been at the forefront of providing help for their families in times of need. Evidence exists to support the idea that grandparents should be considered within a historical context as a vital resource to support the stabilizing effects of family on society-at-large. The purpose of this review is to assess the intervention of grandparents raising grandchildren as an extended family solution to a rapidly growing problem in America.

DEMOGRAPHICS OF GRANDPARENTS RAISING GRANDCHILDREN

Several terms are used in the literature to refer to grandparents raising grandchildren. Among them are "surrogate parenting," "co-parenting," "co-resident parenting," and, the more commonly used, "custodial grandparenting" (Hayslip & Kaminski, 2005; Szinovacz, DeViney, & Atkinson, 1999). The term "custodial grandparenting" is sometimes used in reference to care recognized through the legal system, and, sometimes to describe grandparents providing full-time care for grandchildren without reference to legal rights and benefits. The lack of a single, formal designation clouds the legal and financial issues facing grandparents who take on the roles of parents, and makes it difficult to get precise measures of the extent of this growing phenomenon (Grant, 2000).

The number of grandparents raising grandchildren in America has risen significantly over the last two decades: over 6 million children (6.3% of all children) are receiving primary care from grandparents (4.5 million) or other relatives (1.5 million). This growing total represents a 30 percent increase over the 1990 Census (Smith & Beltran,

2003), which had shown a 44 percent increase over the 1980 Census (Cox, 2000a). Currently, 2.4 million grandparents (8.3% of all grandparents) have primary responsibility for all basic needs of their grandchildren, and 34 percent of the grandparents are accomplishing this without a parent of the grandchild in the home (Cox, 2000a). Census data provided by AARP (2006) show that the grandparent-grandchild arrangement is not evenly distributed within the national population based on percentages of race representation: of the 2.4 million grandparents, 47 percent are white (non-Hispanic), 29 percent are African-American, 17 percent are Hispanic/Latino, 3 percent are Asian, 2 percent are Native American, and 2 percent are classified as other.[1]

Five types of families of grandparents raising grandchildren have been identified: (1) both grandparents, middle generation present; (2) both grandparents, no middle generation present ("skipped generation"; Hooyman & Kiyak, 2005, p. 325); (3 & 4) grandmother only, with and without middle generation presence (Lavers-Preston & Sonuga-Barke, 2003); and, (5) grandfather only (Casper & Bryson, 1998; cited by Cox, 2000a; Glass & Huneycutt, 2002a). The largest of the categories is comprised of both grandparents, with some middle generation representation in the home (1 above), closely followed by grandmother only, with some middle generation representation (3 above). The number of grandparent-grandchild families in each category has increased in size over the last two decades, with the largest growth in the grandfather only category (5 above). Twice as many grandmothers as grandfathers heading households with grandchildren (5 to 3 ratio; Smith & Beltran, 2003, p. 8) is problematic; data exist showing that grandmothers are more likely to live in poverty, rely on public assistance, and have no health insurance (Casper & Bryson, 1998; cited by Cox, 2000a). Indeed, Kelley, Whitley, Sipe, and Yorker (2000) found inadequate social support, lack of resources and poor physical health to be a recipe for psychological distress in grandmothers. Moreover, most grandparent-headed households are located in urban areas of southern states, with the head(s) of the household pos-

---

1. In the United States these percentages vary by state (AARP, 2006). In South Carolina, where the author lives, 51,755 citizens are custodial grandparents with primary care for a grandchild or grandchildren; 42 percent of these are White, 55 percent are African-American, 1 percent are Hispanic/Latino, 2 percent are other. Further, custodial grandparents in South Carolina are more likely to be living in poverty (24%) compared to the national poverty rate for custodial grandparents (19%). These comparisons are important in highlighting the need for tailored services to address regional differences.

sessing less than a high school education (Glass & Huneycutt, 2002a).
In almost half the cases of grandparents raising grandchildren, the
extent of the custodial care is longer than six months, and in one-fifth
of the cases the children remain under the care of a grandparent for
longer than ten years (Grant, 2000).

CAUSES AND EFFECTS OF GRANDPARENTS RAISING GRANDCHILDREN

Grandparental involvement with grandchildren has always
occurred primarily as a result of behavior of the middle generation
(Apple, 1956; Neugarten & Weinstein, 1964; Vann, 2004). Some of the
factors examined and found to influence grandparent-grandchild
interaction are gender (Roberto & Stroes, 1992), race (Pruchno, 1999),
geographic proximity (Tinsley & Parke; 1987), health and age of
grandparents (Kivett, 1985), and whether grandparents perceive positive benefits from interactions with grandchildren (Chan & Elder,
2000). The purpose of the present review, however, is to assess a specific type of grandparent-grandchild relationship, that of grandparents
thrust by default into becoming primary caregivers for grandchildren.

A large number of factors have been demonstrated to influence the
rapid rise in the phenomenon of grandparents raising grandchildren.
Because this type of crisis care involves social problems that often
overlap with poverty, the grandparent-grandchild households are
"increasingly a feature of family structure in low income communities"
(Grant, 2000, p. 18). In addition, all of the factors discussed here effectively include a family crisis involving the loss or incapacitation of a
child for a grandparent (Hayslip & Shore, 2000). As such, the burden
for the grandparent adapting to changes associated with the new role
must be carried while the grandparent is grieving (Cox, 2000a).

The substance abuse epidemic in the United States has been identified as the leading cause of the formation of grandparent-headed
households (Glass & Huneycutt, 2002b) and exerts influence in several ways: drug abuse (including alcohol-abuse) has been shown to ren-
der users incapable of providing consistent nurturance necessary for
effective parenting (Pinson-Millburn, Fabian, Schlossberg, & Pyle,
1996); drug abuse is associated with HIV/AIDS and subsequent incapacitation and/or death of the parent; strict drug laws and mandatory

sentencing have resulted in high rates of incarceration for offenders. The rate of incarceration for women rose six-fold from 1986–1996. Data show that, when mothers are incarcerated, over 50 percent of children reside with grandparents as compared to 20 percent of children who reside with fathers and/or other relatives (U.S. Department of Justice, 1997; U.S. Department of Justice, 1994).

Other circumstances identified as influencing grandparents to accept responsibility to raise grandchildren include divorce, mental or physical impairment of the parent, child abuse/abandonment, and, to a lesser degree, parental death (Hayslip & Shore, 2000; Herrenkohl, Herrenkohl, Rupert, Egolf, & Lutz, 1995). Smith and Beltran (2003) noted that parental death due to terrorism, wars, and natural disasters affects family structures and results in intergenerational caregivers.

Teenage pregnancy (adolescent mothering) also determines family structure, as multigenerational families pool resources to share childrearing duties (Chase-Lansdale, Brooks-Gunn, & Zamsky, 1994). Less than 25 percent of biological fathers of babies born to teenagers live in the home of the mother or provide consistent care for an infant (Oyserman, Radin, & Benn, 1993). This is particularly tragic given the abundance of research showing that nurturing fathers positively influence the social and cognitive development of young children, both directly (Easterbrook & Goldberg, 1984), and indirectly, by influencing maternal interactions (Cowan & Cowan, 1987). Clearly, opportunities exist for grandparents, particularly involved grandfathers, to assume a surrogate father position in the family and significantly impact the lives of grandchildren (Oyserman, Radin, & Benn, 1993).

OUTCOMES FOR GRANDPARENTS AND GRANDCHILDREN

Grandparents have been studied for decades as an important resource for families and parents raising children, but, the circumstances of custodial grandparenting thrust upon older adults in the modern era represent a unique set of societal problems for families and grandparent-grandchild interactions (Grant, 2000; Kornhaber, 1985). The costs for grandparents who accept the challenge of raising grandchildren are considerable and extend beyond obvious financial concerns, social, interpersonal, and health areas of function (Hayslip & Kaminski, 2005). Social disruption occurs as caregivers report isolation from peers and less private time (Jendrek, 1994). The often, unexpected, challenge of custodial grandparenting creates role overload, particularly for young grandparents who still work full-time. Many grandparents, particularly grandmothers, report having to cut back on work hours or quit working altogether when the grandchild(ren) come to stay. Receiving financial public assistance (if available) for surrogate parenting can be stigmatizing for individuals who have always taken pride in their work (Glass & Huneycutt, 2002b). Role confusion occurs for grandparents who suddenly find themselves providing traditional parent care when they had anticipated playing only a peripheral role in the care of grandchildren (Emick & Hayslip, 1999). Further confusion and conflict occur for grandparents when ineffectual and inconsistent parents (the middle generation) exert legal rights to force grandparenting outcomes.

Legal custody of a grandchild can become a formidable issue for grandparents who have to challenge the competency of the biological parent—usually their daughter. Because courts often support the reunification of the parent-child bond against the advice of professionals, custody granted a grandparent can be "lost" at a later point in time, resulting in instability of the household.[2]

Physical and mental health problems are commonly reported for grandparents raising grandchildren (Marx & Solomon, 2000; Strawbridge, Wallhagen, Shema, & Kaplan, 1997). Physical ailments, such as back problems and fatigue, result from everyday tasks such as lifting and carrying the children, over half of whom are less than age six (Glass & Huneycutt, 2002a). The incidence of insomnia, diabetes, and hypertension are greater for custodial grandparents. Anxiety disorders occur when grandparents are overwhelmed by thoughts of guilt and self-blame for what they might have done differently to avoid the problems the parent of the grandchild experienced (Glass & Huneycutt, 2002a). Grandparents worry obsessively about possibilities that grandchildren in their care will be tempted and succumb to the same pressures that killed or incapacitated their parents (Glass & Huneycutt, 2002a). Depression results from despair over the loss of future dreams and goals, leisure activities, social opportunities, and financial independence (Cox, 2000a). Gone for many surrogate parents are oppor-

---

2. A decrease in the number of licensed foster care homes during the 1980s and 1990s has prompted jurisdictions to increasingly consider placing children and grandchildren with relatives (Hegar, 1999; cited by Smith & Beltran, 2003). This growing trend reportedly represents a "paradigm shift" for custodial care (Smith & Beltran, 2003, p. 10).

tunities for generativity typically associated with grandparenting in later life (Fisher, 1995).

Costs and pressures for grandchildren raised by grandparents are equally daunting although some research suggests that children raised in the homes of kin fare better than children placed out of the family (Glass & Huneycutt, 2002a). In addition to problems for grandchildren, including learning disabilities, hyperactivity, HIV-infection, developmental delays, and physical and mental retardation related to parental drug use, are pressures of family upheaval and stigmatization by school peers (Cooley & Unger, 1991; Pinson-Millburn et al., 1996). Emotional problems of anger, confusion, depression, abandonment, and anxiety result for children considered "the walking wounded" as a result of early experiences leading to placement with a grandparent (Glass & Huneycutt, 2002a; p. 154). The problem of ineffective parenting by grandparents can also affect social skill development of grandchildren, and influence the degree to which aggressive behavior and antisocial tendencies are transmitted across generations (Vann, 2004).

PROGRAM AND SERVICE NEEDS OF GRANDPARENTS RAISING GRANDCHILDREN

The rise in the number of surrogate grandparents in America has occurred very rapidly, leaving families and society unprepared (Glass & Huneycutt, 2002a). Grandparents are often faced with choices that must be made quickly, with little or no time to prepare; earlier parenting experiences may not have prepared a grandparent to raise a child who has temporarily or permanently lost a parent (Hayslip & Kaminski, 2005).

Comprehensive programs proving beneficial for custodial grandparents have operated under the construct of levels of intervention (Danish, 1981), and include efforts directed to culture (society), community, and individuals (Hayslip & Kaminski, 2005). Among the topics asked for by grandparents (Watson & Koblinsky, 1997) and included as areas of focus for education and service intervention are financial and legal concerns, child care, school-related issues, medical insurance, and counseling for children and grandparents (Hooyman & Kiyak, 2005, p. 329).

Financial programs include legislative initiatives and advocacy programs to benefit families (Hooyman & Kiyak, 2005, pp. 327–329). For example, the Personal Responsibility Act of 1996 replaced Aid to Families with Dependent Children (AFDC) with the Temporary Assistance for Needy Families Program (TANF), which now requires teen mothers desiring benefits to have a job, be in school, and/or live with parents. Programs such as this have proven beneficial; teen pregnancy has decreased significantly over the last decade across all ethnic groups (35% overall from 1991 to 2005; teenpregnancy.org, 2006), placing fewer infants at risk and fewer grandparents into surrogate parenting roles. In addition, as the result of specifically-focused advocacy efforts, policy makers are increasingly recognizing the need to "support grandparents as sole caregivers outside the traditional foster care or TANF programs" (Hooyman & Kiyak, 2005, p. 328). Other financial areas of concern are housing programs, food stamps, and foster care program payments.[3]

Legal issues for families include assistance with adoption, guardianship and legal custody issues. Though grandparents may know of abuses that have occurred in the family, obtaining legal custody of a grandchild can be a lengthy and costly process, with the burden on grandparents to prove their "fitness" to become surrogate parents. Courts typically evaluate fitness based on issues of financial stability and past and present relationships of grandparents with their children (Glass & Huneycutt, 2002b).[4]

Housing concerns for grandparents are important as space problems can result from the unexpected growth of the family unit. Eviction-related problems are particularly important, as many housing options for older adults do not allow custodial care for grandchildren within the home (Glass & Huneycutt, 2002b). Special issues, such as housing discrimination, have been identified for custodial grandparents who are renters (Fuller-Thomson & Minkler, 2003).

School-related issues also are important and must be addressed in programs developed to aid custodial grandparents. In many jurisdic-

---

3. The Foster Grandparent Program initiated in 1965 allows lower-income elders (60 and older) to receive a financial stipend (federally-funded) for assistance (minimum of 20 hours per week) with special and exceptional needs children (e.g., mentally retarded, handicapped, etc.; Fisher, 1995; Szinovacz & Roberts, 1998).
4. It is possible now in some states for grandparents to receive benefits without legal custody. This requires, however, a written, notarized document from the parent confirming the grandparent's actions on the parent's behalf. The drawback of increased vulnerability for the grandparent is obvious (Glass & Huneycutt, 2002b).

tions, under assumptions that surrogate parenting is a temporary arrangement, grandparents as primary caregivers lack basic rights of parents to register and monitor progress of children in school programs. School-based services such as social work interventions with children displaying behavior problems may be denied family members other than legally designated guardians (Glass & Huneycutt, 2002b).

Childcare issues such as cost and availability of day care and baby sitters for working grandparents are similar to issues for parents and need to be addressed effectively. Similarly, schools and medical insurers (public and private) need the legal power to recognize authority of grandparents for medical decision-making and recommendations for remedial education and testing for grandchildren (Glass & Huneycutt, 2002b).

Counseling challenges for children and grandparents include psychosocial grief interventions and programs aimed at effective management of emotional disturbance (Pinson-Millburn et al., 1996). Possibilities exist to educate and train grandparents in filial therapy to become "therapeutic agents" in the life of the grandchild (Bratton, Ray, & Moffit, 1998). Filial therapy assumes that family members with a deep understanding of a child, who displays behavioral and emotional problems, can learn techniques to create a safe and non-judgmental environment where the child can successfully cope with grief and stresses of adjustment. Stress management for children, parents, and grandparents is increasingly included in intervention efforts involving counseling (Burnette, 1998; Pinson-Millburn, et al., 1996). Respite programs, support groups and grandparent education initiatives have proven particularly beneficial (Cohen & Pyle, 2000; Glass & Huneycutt, 2002a; Hayslip & Kaminski, 2005). Education concerning management of neurological and behavioral problems resulting from prenatal drug abuse (including hyperactivity) is beneficial, as are programs to counteract domestic violence and educate young parents concerning stresses of parenthood.

In summary, programs and services need to address all of the aforementioned issues to offer grandparents as caregivers every opportunity available to provide children in their care normal social and cognitive opportunities. Examples of education curricula for eight-class and twelve-class programs are available in the professional literature (Burnette, 1998; Cox, 2000b; Vacha-Haase, Ness, Dannison, & Smith,

2000). In addition, publications are available that offer custodial grandparents useful information, such as advice on record-keeping needs and how to assess whether hiring a lawyer is worth the expense (Glass & Huneycutt, 2002b) to descriptions of parent skills training programs (Hayslip & Kaminski, 2005) and intergenerational programs (Szinovacz & Roberts, 1998, pp. 250–253).

FUTURE DIRECTIONS

Grandparents will continue to provide crisis care for their loved ones, and every effort needs to be undertaken by professionals and members of the larger community to identify and provide assistance for diverse families at risk (Kivett, 1993). Research and education at all levels have proven beneficial and creative interventions are being tested and reported each day. The mentality of the extended family seems particularly useful in this regard and inclusion of all family members (including nonbiological relatives, called fictive kin; Lemme, 2006, p. 280) will result in the identification of best practices. Lists and descriptions of innovative programs and resources are extensive and available (AARP, 2006; Cox, 2000b; Roe, 2000; Szinovacz & Roberts, 1998).

The media in any community can be valuable allies in raising awareness of issues of custodial grandparenting (Roe, 2000). The wide reach of newspapers and television, and, for a new generation of responsive advocates, Internet website links, and blogs, can influence system-level decision makers, such as politicians and visionary businesspersons. Practical programming aimed at professionals and families can provide strategic help and links to isolated caregivers (Roe, 2000). Pruchno (1999) used the media to recruit subjects for research comparing experiences of black and white grandmothers raising grandchildren and reported that 70 percent of participants "learned about the study primarily through media press releases" (p. 211).

New technologies for communication, such as webcasting and videoconferencing, are reaching into previously inaccessible areas to deliver practical course content to caregivers. Conferences and professional journals are increasingly promoted and held online, allowing for region-to-region and cross-cultural communication in a low-cost format not available to previous generations. Researchers and practitioners routinely use email for rapid and efficient data transmission of up-to-the-minute information on what works and what doesn't.

Churches, synagogues, mosques, schools, and civic organizations are increasingly getting into the picture as "supporting communities" to promote the grandparenting movement. Working at the grassroots level for development of educational and service programs, community members are reaching beyond their own defined needs and boundaries to interact with other like-minded persons and organizations. This systems approach toward "framing the central issues as those of a healthy community rather than merely the problems of individual families" (Roe, 2000, p. 294) will no doubt impact individuals, families, and communities of the future.

REFERENCES

AARP (American Association of Retired Persons). (2006). *Grandparenting: State specific data and information.* Retrieved: May 11, 2007, http://www.aarp.org/families/grandparents/.

Albrecht, R. (1954). The parental responsibilities of grandparents. *Marriage and Family Living, 16,* 201–204.

Apple, D. (1956). The social structure of grandparenthood. *American Anthropologist, 58*(4), 656–663.

Bratton, S., Ray, D., & Moffit, K. (1998). Filial/family play therapy: An intervention for custodial grandparents and their grandchildren. *Educational Gerontology, 24*(4), 391–406.

Burnette, D. (1998). Grandparents rearing grandchildren: A school-based small group intervention. *Research on Social Work Practice, 8*(1), 10–27.

Casper, L.M., & Bryson, K.R. (1998). Co-resident grandparents and their grandchildren: Grandparent maintained families. *Population Division Working Paper*, No. 26. Washington, D.C.: U.S. Bureau of the Census.

Chan, C.G., & Elder, G.H., Jr. (2000). Matrilineal advantage in grandchild-grandparent relations. *The Gerontologist, 40*(2), 179–190.

Chase-Lansdale, P.L., Brooks-Gunn, J., & Zamsky, E.S. (1994). Young African-American multigenerational families in poverty: Quality of mothering and grandmothering. *Child Development, 65,* 373–393.

Cherlin, A., & Furstenberg, F. (1986). Grandparents and family crisis. *Generations, 10,* 26–28.

Cohen, C.S., & Pyle, R. (2000). Support groups in the lives of grandmothers raising grandchildren. In C.B. Cox (Ed.), *To grandmother's house we go and stay* (pp. 235–252). New York: Springer.

Cooley, M.L., & Unger, D.G. (1991). The role of family support in determining developmental outcomes in children of teen mothers. *Child Psychiatry and Human Development, 21*(3), 217–234.

Cowan, C.P., & Cowan, P.A. (1987). Men's involvement in parenthood. In P.W. Berman & F.A. Pederson (Eds.), *Men's transitions to parenthood* (pp. 145–174). Hillsdale, NJ: Erlbaum.

Cox, C.B. (2000a). Why grandchildren are going to and staying at grandmother's house and what happens when they get there. In C.B. Cox (Ed.), *To grandmother's house we go and stay* (pp. 3-19). New York: Springer.

Cox, C.B. (2000b). Empowering grandparents raising grandchild. In C.B. Cox (Ed.), *To grandmother's house we go and stay* (pp. 253-267). New York: Springer.

Danish, S. (1981). Life span development and intervention: A necessary link. *Counseling Psychology, 9*, 40–43.

Easterbrook, M.A., & Goldberg, W.A. (1984). Toddler development in the family: Impact of father involvement and parental characteristics. *Child Development, 55*, 740–752.

Emick, M.A., & Hayslip, B., Jr. (1999). Custodial grandparenting: Stresses, coping skills, and relationships with grandchildren. *International Journal of Aging and Human Development, 48*(1), 35–61.

Fisher, B. (1995). Successful aging, life satisfaction, and generativity in later life. *International Journal of Aging and Human Development, 41*(3), 239–250.

Fuller-Thomson, E., & Minkler, M. (2003). Housing issues and realities facing grandparent caregivers who are renters. *The Gerontologist, 43*(1), 92–98.

Glass, J.C., Jr., & Huneycutt, T.L. (2002a). Grandparents parenting grandchildren: Extent of situation, issues involved, and educational implications. *Educational Gerontology, 28*, 139–161.

Glass, J.C., Jr., & Huneycutt, T.L. (2002b). Grandparents raising grandchildren: The courts, custody, and educational implications. *Educational Gerontology, 28*, 237–251.

Grant, R. (2000). The special needs of children in kinship care. *Journal of Gerontological Social Work, 33*(3), 17–33.

Harbert, A.S., & Ginsberg, L.H. (1990). *Human services for older adults: Concepts and skills* (2nd ed.). Columbia, SC: University of South Carolina Press.

Hayslip, B., Jr., & Shore, R.J. (2000). Custodial grandparenting and mental health services. *Journal of Mental Health and Aging, 6*(4), 367–383.

Hayslip, B., Jr., & Kaminski, P.L. (2005). Grandparents raising their grandchildren: A review of the literature and suggestions for practice. *The Gerontologist, 45*(2), 262–269.

Hegar, R.L. (1999). Kinship foster care: The new child placement paradigm. In R.L. Hegar & M. Scannapieco (Eds.), *Kinship foster care* (pp. 225–238). New York: Oxford University Press.

Herrenkohl, E.C., Herrenkohl, R.C., Rupert, L.J., Egolf, B.P., & Lutz, J.G. (1995). Risk factors for behavioral dysfunction: The relative impact of maltreatment, SES, physical health problems, cognitive ability, and quality of parent-child interaction. *Child Abuse & Neglect, 19*(2), 191–203.

Hooyman, N.R., & Kiyak, H.A. (2005). Social gerontology: A multidisciplinary perspective (7th ed.). Boston: Pearson Education.

Jendrek, M.P. (1994). Grandparents who parent their grandchildren: Circumstances and decisions. *The Gerontologist, 34*(2), 206–216.

Kahana, E., & Kahana, B. (1971). Theoretical and research perspectives on grand-parenthood. *Aging and Human Development, 2*, 261–268.

Kelley, S.J., Whitley, D., Sipe, T.A., & Yorker, B.C. (2000). Psychological distress in grandmother kinship care providers: The role of resources, social support, and physical health. *Child Abuse & Neglect, 24*(3), 311–321.

Kivett, V.R. (1985). Grandfathers and grandchildren: Patterns of association, help-ing, and psychological closeness. *Family Relations, 34*, 565–571.

Kivett, V.R. (1993). Racial comparisons of the grandmother role: Implications for strengthening the family support system of older black women. *Family Relations, 42*(2), 165–172.

Kornhaber, A. (1985). Grandparenting: Normal and pathological—A preliminary communication from The Grandparent Study. Scientific Meeting of the Boston Society for Gerontologic Psychiatry. (April 13).

Lavers-Preston, C.A., & Sonuga-Barke, E.J. (2003). An intergenerational perspective on parent-child relationships: The reciprocal effects of tri-generational grandpar-ent-parent-child relationships. In J. Gupta & D. Parry-Gupta (Eds.), *Children & parents: Clinical issues for psychologists and psychiatrists*, (pp. 155–179). Philadelphia: Whurer Publications, Ltd.

Lemme, B.H. (2006). Development in adulthood (4th ed.). Boston: Pearson Educa-tion.

Marx, J., & Solomon, J.C. (2000). Physical health of custodial grandparents. In C.B. Cox (Ed.), *To grandmother's house we go and stay* (pp. 37–55). New York: Springer.

Neugarten, B.L., & Weinstein, K.K. (1964). The changing American grandparent. *Journal of Marriage and the Family, 26*(2), 199–204.

Oyserman, D., Radin, N., & Benn, R. (1993). Dynamics in a three-generational fam-ily: Teens, grandparents, and babies. *Developmental Psychology, 29*(3), 564–572.

Pinson-Millburn, N.M., Fabian, E.S., Schlossberg, N.K., & Pyle, M. (1996). Grandparents raising grandchildren. *Journal of Counseling & Development, 74*, 548–554.

Pruchno, R. (1999). Raising grandchildren: The experiences of black and white grandmothers. *The Gerontologist, 39*(2), 209–221.

Roberto, K.A., & Stroes, J. (1992). Grandchildren and grandparents: Roles, Influences, and Relationships. *International Journal of Aging and Human Development, 34*, 227–239.

Roe, K.M. (2000). Community interventions to support grandparent caregivers: Lessons learned from the field. In C.B. Cox (Ed.), To grandmother's house we go and stay (pp. 283–303). New York: Springer.

Smith, C.J., & Beltran, A. (2003). The role of federal policies in supporting grand-parents raising grandchildren families: The case of the U.S. *Journal of Intergenerational Relationships, 1*(2), 5–20.

Strawbridge, W. J., Wallhagen, M.I., Shema, S.J., & Kaplan, G.A. (1997). New bur-dens or more of the same? Comparing grandparent, spouse, and adult-child care-givers. *The Gerontologist, 37*(4), 505–510.

Szinovacz, M.E. (1998). Grandparent research: Past, present, and future. In M.E. Szi-novacz (Ed.), *Handbook on grandparenthood* (pp. 2–20). Westport, CT: Greenwood.

Szinovacz, M.E., & Roberts, A. (1998). Programs for grandparents. In M.E. Szinovacz (Ed.), *Handbook on grandparenthood* (pp. 247–256). Westport, CT: Greenwood.

Szinovacz, M.E., DeViney, S., & Atkinson, M.P. (1999). Effects of surrogate parenting on grandparents' well-being. *Journal of Gerontology: Series B: Psychological Sciences and Social Sciences, 54B*(6), S376–S388.

Teenpregnancy.org: Research, resources and information. (2006). *General facts and statistics.* Retrieved: May 15, 2007, http://www.teenpregnancy.org/resources/data/genlfact.asp.

Tinsley, B.R., & Parke, R.D. (1987). Grandparents as interactive and social support agents for families with young infants. *International Journal of Aging and Human Development, 25*(4), 259–277.

U.S. Department of Justice. (1994). *Bureau of Justice Statistics special report: Women in prison.* (Publication No. NCJ-145321). Washington, DC: U.S. Government Printing Office.

U.S. Department of Justice. (1997). Prisoners in 1996. (Report No. NCJ-164619). Washington, DC: Bureau of Justice Statistics.

Vacha-Haase, T., Ness, C.M., Dannison, L., & Smith, A. (2000). Grandparents raising grandchildren: A psychoeducational group approach. *Journal for Specialists in Group Work, 25*(1), 67–78.

Vann, M.S. (2004). Grandparenting as a functional experience within the extended family. *Dissertation Abstracts International: Section B: The Sciences and Engineering, 65*(11-B), 6035.

Von Hentig, H. (1946). The sociological function of the grandmother. *Social Forces, 24,* 389–392.

Watson, J.A., & Koblinsky, S.A. (1997). Strengths and needs of working-class African-American and Anglo-American grandparents. *International Journal of Aging and Human Development, 44*(2), 149–165.

Part II

ROLES AND RESPONSIBILITIES OF THE AMERICAN FAMILY

Not only has the family undergone significant change in terms of definition and make up, it continues in its transformation in terms of its roles and responsibilities in the American society. Some of these changes can be seen in the way the American culture itself has evolved, e.g., in terms of gender roles and how this evolution has had impact on the traditional way that women and men relate to one another in the context of the family. Indeed, the male-dominated household, if not more rare than common, at least is not dominant in the way that it once was in American society.

In addition to differences that gender plays in the American family today, families continue to be society's primary delivery system for everything from matters that pertain to education, childrearing, child development and health, to the passing on of family and cultural traditions. In this light, the family is expected to embrace both old and new as societal expectations continue to change.

Parents and guardians have a significant responsibility to assist their children in being positioned for success in school and beyond. Clearly this is no easy task as society's distractions and intrusions continue to grow in number and complexity. And, society's definition of success continues to undergo change as well. While the power of the accountability movement in the United States cannot be taken lightly, no reasonable individual would conclude that success on standardized tests can be translated automatically into success in society.

In addition to formal schooling, the American family can, or at least should, play an important role in the health of its members, in particular its young members. This can be seen in the family's influence on everything from diet, to exercise, to self-concept and personal well being. Beyond merely setting a good example for another, the role of family members in assisting in the healthy development of other family members includes jointly engaging in positive health practices and not just giving lip service to these behaviors.

Finally, through oral narrative, whether by design or by the mere influence of simply being in a family environment, the family influences how individuals see themselves, how they accept or take on their individual roles in the family and in society at large, and how they understand and eventually pass on to others their personal and family traditions. Narrative within the family is an important communication tool that has long-lasting impact on individuals from their early development to later adult years.

The readings in this section include discussions of the role of gender in the American family and the role that the family should play in the education and healthy development of its members. Also included is discussion of childrearing practices in the family, in particular as these have been influenced historically by noted American psychologists. The readings conclude with a discussion of oral narrative in the family in terms of how individuals see themselves, the roles that they assume in the family and in society, and how oral narrative influences the understanding and passing on of family traditions and the actual definition of family itself.

Chapter 6

JUSTICE IN THE FAMILY

Julinna C. Oxley and Nils Ch. Rauhut

HISTORY OF JUSTICE AND THE NATURE OF THE FAMILY

Is the traditional family a just social institution? Although this question is an important one, most political philosophers of the past have not addressed it.[1] The reasons for this neglect are relatively easy to understand. The main reason is that political thinkers have drawn a distinction between the public and the private realms of life. The standard view is that the public realm is characterized by conflict, competition, scarcity of resources, and the pursuit of self-interest. If left unregulated by strong principles of justice, the public realm is in danger of disintegrating into a state of war and anarchy. The private realm, on the other hand, is seen as the sphere of love and compassion. In private relationships, people tend to cooperate and perform genuine acts of altruism. The private sphere, therefore, does not need to be regulated by principles of justice. All it needs is protection from state and public intrusion. Since family life is the central element of the private sphere, most political philosophers conclude that the family simply

---

1. The two notable exceptions in the history of Western Philosophy are Plato and John Stuart Mill. Plato argued in Book V of the *Republic* that the nuclear family is incompatible with the life and upbringing of the most talented men and women in the ideal and just society. John Stuart Mill, on the other hand, argued in his book *The Subjection of Women* that the subordination of women within the family is incompatible with the wider political equality of women in society. Mill was especially concerned that young men would grow up thinking that, in virtue of being born male, they are superior to "all and every one of an entire half of the human race."

needs some form of legal protection, and that family life does not need to be regulated by the same principles of justice that regulate the public sphere of life.

A second reason for neglecting the justice of the family is that many political philosophers (such as John Locke) have argued that families are *natural* social institutions. The division of labor within families, in which women are assigned the role of doing most of the domestic labor (including childrearing), and where men are assigned the role of providing resources and protection for the family, is seen as the result of natural differences between men and women. It is argued that women, by nature, find greater fulfillment in childrearing and that men, by nature, find greater joy in competing for resources in the more competitive public world. As long as this unequal division of labor within families is seen as a result of unavoidable biological destiny, the unequal distribution of burdens and opportunities for men and women do not need to be evaluated in light of principles of justice.

In recent years, a significant number of feminist Anglo-American philosophers have come to challenge these assumptions about the traditional family. They argue that families are anything but naturally ordered institutions and point out that states already regulate who can marry, who has parental rights, who can divorce, and on what terms they can divorce. Moreover, in many nations, the legal framework for family life has undergone a tremendous transformation during the last two hundred years. These observations point to two conclusions. First, it seems false to claim that families only belong to a private, prepolitical realm. The state already plays a crucial role in ordering and shaping family life. Families should be understood as political institutions that need to be evaluated according to principles of justice. Second, the transformation of the legal framework for family life indicates that the structure of family life is not ordered merely by nature, but also by social conventions. It follows, therefore, that traditional family life and the resulting division of labor within families needs to be assessed in terms of contemporary theories of justice. In the following essay, we will focus on the work by the political theorist Susan Moller Okin. Her book, *Justice, Gender, and the Family*, was the first to give a systematic treatment of justice and the modern American family.[2]

---

2. *Justice, Gender, and the Family*, Basic Books, 1989. All references to this book will be cited internally.

THE INJUSTICE OF TRADITIONAL FAMILIES

Okin's analysis of the modern American family consists of three main areas: first, an evaluation of marriage and familial relationships and the division of labor in raising children in contemporary American families; second, a negative critique of contemporary American political theorists' treatment of the nature and role of the family; and, third, the development of her own theory of how to achieve justice in the family. We will begin by summarizing her views in the first two areas in this section; section three will contain a detailed analysis of her views on how to achieve just families.

Okin's thesis is that American families in the twentieth century are *unjust* institutions (135). She argues that there are "substantial inequalities" between the sexes in our society, and that "underlying all these inequalities is the unequal distribution of the unpaid labor of the family" (25). Okin distinguishes between paid (or productive) and unpaid (or reproductive) labor, and then shows that, in American households, there are few in which both parents perform the unpaid labor. Two-fifths of married women in America are full-time housewives. They work 49.3 hours a week, while the employed husband works 63.2 hours. In the households in which the wife works part-time (less than 30 hours a week), she still works 40 hours a week in the home (150). Employed wives, according to Okin, still do the greatest proportion of unpaid family work, including housework and child care. A quarter of the children in the United States live in families with only one parent, and in 90 percent of the cases, this is with the mother (4). These women are much more likely to be in low-paying jobs that do not have benefits and are never acknowledged as having other "work" at home to do.

The problem, says Okin, is that the women in each of these situations are at a serious disadvantage. The women who are housewives are dependent on their husbands and less able to support themselves, because their labor is unpaid. Their work is devalued because it is not paid, and it is never really acknowledged as work *or* as productive, at least in terms of monetary renumeration (151). Since the housewife's work does not give her access to much money, her situation can be humiliating, especially where she must ask for money to run the household or buy things for herself. In this case, the distribution of benefits (including basic security) disfavors the member of the family who doesn't earn income outside of the home. The situation of divorced or never-married mothers is worse, for they must support themselves *and* their children. The economic situation of women after divorce generally plummets, while that of a divorced man usually is better than when he was married. These factors contribute to the "feminization of poverty," due to the fact that single women with children are becoming poorer because they get little support from the fathers of the children.

In these situations of injustice, Okin argues that the inequality in the family is directly linked to gender socialization and inequalities. She observes that the disparity within the family is due to the gender structure of the family, which is historically and socially constructed. This structure is ultimately based on a sexual division of labor, in which beliefs about the role of women in the family still permeate our society, and that these beliefs about sexual difference are deeply entrenched in the social relations and roles in families today (5–6). Contemporary families are the "lynchpin of gender, reproducing it from one generation to the next" (170). But, Okin says that the problem isn't just simply that women are dominated by a patriarchal system; rather, women have learned to take time off of work, move because of their husbands' careers, and take jobs that are less demanding so as to spend time with the family. The result is that there is a cycle of inequality that is perpetuated in the family, when women perform unpaid labor and fail to demand that the other partner contribute equally. This is the "cycle of vulnerability," whereby the "heavy weight of tradition, combined with the effects of socialization, still works powerfully to reinforce sex roles that are commonly regarded as of unequal prestige and worth" (6). But she says, "surely nothing in our natures dictates that men should not be equal participants in the rearing of their children" (5). Okin argues that it is only women's socialization, and not their natures, that leads them to be primary caregivers who are often overworked and never genuinely paid.

Although Okin thinks that contemporary American families are unjust, she thinks that the family is a central part of children's moral development and, instead of abolishing it or outsourcing the labor to other individuals, the family is a school of justice that simply needs attention and reform. Her main claim is that the family must be just because of the vast influence that it has on the moral development of children (17). She suggests that, unless children experience justice and reciprocity in the home, rather than domination and manipulation, and unless they are treated with concern and respect, they will be hindered in their moral development in being able to follow principles of justice (17). The family is central to a child's moral development, and, in order for children to learn to be just, they must live in just families where the two partners divide the reproductive labor equally so that they do not take advantage of the mother's free labor.

Okin also points out that the gender structure of the family contributes to inequality in the arena of "equal opportunities." While some political theorists emphasize equality of opportunity, she argues that there will never be a genuine equality of opportunity because people are not born as equal individuals in society, but into family situations that are unjust. Gendered roles are perpetuated in the family, and these are obstacles to the equality of opportunity. For example, a girl may be raised to think that her destiny is to become a housekeeper and a mother. She will, as a result, have fewer options for living a satisfied and independent life outside the home. If she has any desire to live a relatively comfortable life, she will seek out a husband who will make money while she provides the domestic labor for the child. The result is that the woman's (diminished) opportunity for getting a job directly corresponds to the dependence on another that she will have in the family. Her workplace potential and her work in the family life are interconnected. "A cycle of power relations and decisions pervades both family and workplace, and the inequalities of each reinforce those that already exist in the other" (147).

This summarizes Okin's leading ideas about the nature of the injustice of the family, which is based on the fact that women are socialized to work for free and never receive credit for what they do. Based on her diagnosis of the modern family and the nature of its injustice, Okin concludes that justice must be achieved in the family. To explain how Okin envisions that justice, we now turn to her positive argument on justice and her adaptation of John Rawls' theory of justice to develop her own theory.

APPLYING JOHN RAWLS' THEORY OF JUSTICE TO THE FAMILY

Okin's solution to the injustice of families involves adapting a leading idea of the American political philosopher John Rawls' political theory—the Original Position. Okin's argument on how to achieve justice in the family is, in part, a feminist response to Rawls' theory of justice, which has been the most influential political theory of the late twentieth and twenty-first centuries. Thus, in order to understand Okin's theory of justice in the family, we will begin by describing the components of Rawls' political theory, and then explain how Okin uses and modifies it in developing her own theory of justice in the family. For the most part, Okin uses Rawls' method of how to deliberate or reason about justice, rather than directly adopting any of the specific principles that Rawls endorses in his theory of justice.

Rawls' *A Theory of Justice* is a theory of justice for social institutions.[3] It is a seminal work in political philosophy, and since it is complex, we will be restricted here to a somewhat cursory overview of his main ideas about justice. Rawls begins with the thesis that the primary subject of justice is the basic structure of society. That is, he thinks that the most important aim of a theory of justice is to describe the principles of justice that are required in order to achieve a just society. He says the situation in which we find ourselves involves both cooperation and conflict. Because we are in such circumstances, we are, therefore, in need of establishing shared rules of conduct which are the principles of justice.

Rawls takes a contractarian approach to deriving and stating the principles of justice; this method aims at the public justification of moral and political principles. His idea is that the principles of justice are the ones that are principles that would be chosen by rational people situated in a kind of "state of nature" which he calls the Original Position. While Rawls emphasizes the contractarian aspects of the theory—the importance of reasonable agreement and shared public reasons—it is couched in the language of rational choice. Thus, Rawls thinks that the choice of the principles of justice must ultimately be rational, which means that the principles would be agreed upon by persons who are seeking to fulfill their own interests. The aim of his theory of justice is to provide a method or a procedure for deliberating about justice, and using this method will result in the choice of a specific conception of justice.

The method that Rawls proposes for deliberating on justice is called the Original Position, which is a description of the *circumstances* in

---

3. Rawls' *A Theory of Justice* was published in 1971, and revised again in 1999, several years before his death. We will quote from the revised version, *A Theory of Justice*, Revised Edition, Harvard University Press, Cambridge, 1999, p. 7. All references to this text will be cited internally.

which the principles of justice should be chosen. The Original Position (OP) is the hypothetical assembly of rational agents whose task is to decide, for everyone in society and for future generations, the principles of justice that are to define just institutional activities and procedures. It is, for us, a procedure for choosing a conception of justice that outlines "the way in which the major social institutions distribute fundamental rights and duties and determine the division of advantages from social cooperation" (6). Rawls says the Original Position is an "expository device" (21) or, essentially, a thought-experiment, designed to describe the ideal circumstances for deliberating about the principles of justice. The device includes (a) procedures of moral decision-making that are widely believed to be "fair," (b) general information believed to be relevant to such deliberations, and (c) the exclusion of information that is morally irrelevant and which leads to bias or special negotiations.

The OP device stipulates various considerations that shape the deliberations of the parties who are situated in the OP. (These parties are generic rational actors.) The constraints guarantee that, whatever choice the parties make, it is just: "The idea of the original position is to set up a fair procedure so that any principles agreed to will be just" (118). These constraints include (1) the motivation of the parties as disinterested, (2) the relationship of the parties as equal, (3) the veil of ignorance, and (4) the sense of justice. Let us begin with the first, the motivation of rational individuals, which means that they are interested in pursuing their own interests, not others'.[4] They are disposed to cooperate with others, but want to choose a social scheme that will insure that their rights in the scheme are equally protected. Assigning the parties this disposition insures that the principles of justice "do not depend upon strong assumptions" (111), for "a conception of justice should not presuppose, then, extensive ties of natural sentiment" (112). Though the parties are assigned this specific disposition, this motivation doesn't seem very robust, for Rawls argues later that the parties' choice would be the same if they had been assigned a benevolent disposition (167). Thus, it seems that the other constraints of the Original Position are more important in shaping the reasoning of the parties.

The second feature is that the parties are placed in an initial position of equality which describes "the fundamental terms of their associa-

---

4. Rawls says that the parties are "assumed to take no interest in one another's interests (although they may have a concern for third parties)" (127).

tion" (10). This means that no one party has greater power or more advantages than another. If the parties were not equal, then some would have bargaining advantages over others, and the result would be that their competing claims would not be ranked at all and the outcome would be "determined by force and cunning" (117). Because no one is inferior to others, and no one is believed to be less worthy of moral respect, then the contractors in the Original Position are forced to regard each other equally in the sense that they each have legitimate claims and expectations. Rather, "each person possesses an inviolability" (3) that society cannot impinge upon, even if it increases its welfare.

The third constraint, the veil of ignorance, conceals each party's specific identity. When someone is behind the veil, she doesn't know her own social status or class position, her racial or cultural background, her conception of the good life, or personality traits, whether she is male or female, or whether she is naturally gifted with strength or intelligence. It is a "thick" veil of ignorance that shields knowledge of the parties' place in history, the circumstances of their economic and democratic relations, etc. Its main function is to prohibit knowledge of one's distinguishing attributes that would motivate a morally arbitrary choice. Eliminating knowledge of these differences provides grounds for the *possibility of agreement*, for it eliminates differences between the contractors, so that they deliberate in the same way. The veil "makes possible a unanimous choice of a particular conception of justice. Without these limitations on knowledge the bargaining problem of the original position would be hopelessly complicated" (121). The presence of the veil of ignorance and the resulting identical deliberations imply that the reasoning of the parties is that of a single individual.[5]

The final condition is that the parties are assumed to be "capable of a sense of justice and this fact is public knowledge among them" (125). The sense of justice means that they are able to "understand and to act in accordance with whatever principles are finally agreed to" and insure that "the principles chosen will be respected" (125). The sense of justice also enables the parties to be reasonable, and to choose a conception of justice that they can plausibly anticipate acting on.

5. Jean Hampton argues further that eliminating these differences prohibits bargaining among the parties. "Contracts and Choices: Does Rawls Have a Social Contract Theory?" *Journal of Philosophy*, JE 80; 77: 315–338.

Though Rawls implies that the sense of justice is formal, since it is a way of stipulating that the parties will take the relevant facts about moral psychology into account when choosing the conception of justice, the idea is that the parties understand what actual agents are capable of doing, given an understanding of their moral personality. They understand what actual agents are capable of learning in terms of justice.

These four features, in combination, model the point of view "from which a fair agreement between free and equal persons can be reached."[6] The parties are *representatives* of free and equal citizens who are to reach an agreement under fair conditions, which is guaranteed by the veil of ignorance.[7] The idea is that, given this way of reasoning about justice, the parties will choose a conception of justice that they could live with, no matter who they turn out to be in society.

So how is this theory of justice interpreted by Okin? She begins by arguing that Rawls only uses the device of the Original Position to think about the requirements of justice as they are applied to social institutions. Rawls never considers the possibility that the family could be a social institution in which the principles of justice apply. In fact, as she notes, the only time that Rawls mentions the family is in his discussion of moral psychology, where he says that children acquire their sense of justice first in the family. It is this aspect of Rawls' argument that Okin agrees with and uses as a point of departure from which to develop her own theory of justice for the family.

Okin's response to Rawls involves making two main arguments about justice and the family. First, she argues that political theorists such as Rawls correctly believe that, as a matter of moral psychology, justice is learned in the family, but, that second, they wrongly assume that the institution of the family is *de facto* just. Rawls is right to emphasize the importance of the family in shaping our ideas about justice, and the fact that a sense of justice will develop in a just family, but, as she shows, the family is not a just institution. For a theory of justice to be complete, Okin asserts that it must include women and must address the gender inequalities that she thinks are prevalent in modern day families. Her solution is to show how the Original Position can

---

6. "Justice as Fairness: Political not Metaphysical," *The Collected Papers of John Rawls,* p. 400.
7. See also "Kantian Constructivism," (*The Collected Papers of John Rawls,* p. 310) where Rawls says that the "original position situates free and equal moral persons fairly with respect to one another."

provide the framework for evaluating *personal* relationships–not just our *political* ones–and for setting out the characteristics of a just family.

Okin's adaptation of the Original Position involves asking what kinds of arrangements would persons in a Rawlsian original position agree to in the matters of marriage, parental and other domestic responsibilities, divorce, and policies in social life (such as the workplace and schools) (174)? She asks the reader to imagine himself in the Original Position, where he doesn't know his sex or other personal characteristics, and, thus, must choose policies that would be fair, because he could turn out to be either one of those sexes once the veil of ignorance is lifted. Particularly relevant, she says, is a lack of knowledge about "our beliefs about the characteristics of men and women and our related convictions about the appropriate division of labor between the sexes" (174). That is, we don't know what we think about gender roles in the family. We may, once the veil is lifted, "find ourselves feminist men or feminist women whose conception of the good life includes the minimization of social differentiation between the sexes." Or, she says, we may "find ourselves traditionalist men or women whose conception of the good life, for religious or other reasons, is bound up in an adherence to the conventional division of labor between the sexes" (Both quotes 174). The aim is to find principles of justice that would satisfy both of these views and the ones in-between.[8] Essentially, she is asking, what kinds of arrangements would be reasonably agreed to, if we did not know which gender we would be in a marriage?

CREATING JUST FAMILIES

Okin's answer to the above question is that the appropriate model of relationship would be one that mimimized gender, but that people who are in gender-structured marriages should be protected. Okin's main argument is that the family should be egalitarian in structure. This primarily involves moving away from traditional gender roles that saddle women with the majority of childrearing labor. She argues that marriages that minimize gender differences and share both pro-

---

8. There are certain traditionalist positions that are "so extreme" that they are not admitted for consideration.

ductive (paid) and reproductive (unpaid) labor are the most desirable, but that the traditionalist forms should also be accepted. According to Okin, a fair society is one that encourages the equal sharing by men and women of paid and unpaid work, of productive, and reproductive labor, and that, in a fair society, public policies should protect the vulnerability of women and children. We will briefly explain her views on how to achieve a genderless marriage (via changes in the workplace and state sanctions), and then outline her recommendations for protecting women in traditional marriages or who are single.

In order to facilitate and encourage equally shared parenting, major changes would need to be made both in the workplace and in schools. These include providing parental leave for both mothers and fathers after the birth of their children, greater flexibility for parents of children with health problems, and on-site day care for parents who work at large-scale employers. The aim is to facilitate shared parenting by encouraging men—as well as women—to take leave during the years in which their children are young (176). In schools, children need to be taught about the "politics of gender," including the inequalities and uncertainties of marriage, and the "likely consequences of making life choices based on assumptions about gender" (177). In addition, schools need to teach boys and girls the same kinds of household activities, as well as provide high-quality after-school programs where children can play safely, and participate in creative activities. Such programs will enable children to be more open and cooperative with other genders. Both married couples and never-married mothers would greatly benefit from a work environment that takes parenthood seriously by subsidizing childcare, and from high-quality daycare in the schools.

While these recommendations are meant to encourage shared parenting, Okin acknowledges that some people will choose to be in gender-structured marriages, or marriages in which one partner works full time while the other stays at home caring for the children. She argues that these relationships are currently "necessary" institutions because they are still chosen by some, and, since they exist, they should be subject "to a number of legal requirements, at least where there are children" (180). Her recommendation is to create a situation in which the division of labor doesn't lead to economic dependence of one partner on another. Her proposal is for both partners to have "equal legal entitlement" to all earnings coming into the household. "The clearest and simplest way of doing this would be to have employers make out wage checks equally divided between the earner and the partner who provides all or most of his or her unpaid domestic services" (181). This is recommended because it would prevent one partner from exploiting his power over the other partner. While some partners may choose to deposit the funds into the same account, and use the monies jointly, such a practice would codify the fact that they agree that the income should be rightly shared. Her point is that the equal splitting of wages would "constitute public recognition of the fact that the currently unpaid labor of families is just as important as the paid labor" (181).

When it comes to separation and divorce, Okin suggests that divorce laws should protect women who have been working domestically in the marriage. She argues that the "terms of exit" from a marriage should be very clear, so that women will not stay in a bad relationship because it will be an "economic catastrophe" (182). The childrearing partners should be entitled to much more than they currently are now, and "both postdivorce households should enjoy the same standard of living" (183). That is, the income should be divided jointly between the spouses so that the children have a standard of living that is just as good as the parent without custody of the children. In addition, never married women with children should also receive support in raising their children. The first measures taken should be to educate people (especially teenagers) about the difficulties of parenthood and the importance of contraception; especially, men need to be encouraged not to have careless sexual behavior that will lead to the responsibility of parenthood. But, in these cases, the paternity should be established in all cases, and rules should be enforced that require fathers to contribute their support to the child. Where the father cannot pay (due to incarceration or otherwise), Okin proposes governmental backup support (178).

It is evident that Okin thinks that the state should play a visible role in regulating justice within families—gendered, egalitarian, divorced, or single. Her proposals for regulating justice within families involve significant state intervention, which is a cause for concern given her "liberal" stance. But, she points out that this regulation is not any more than what currently exists—such as requiring marriage registrations, tax returns, etc.—and thus, is not too intrusive or burdensome. Moreover, the benefits of such regulations are monumental,—"families in which roles and responsibilities are equally shared regardless of sex are far more in accord with principles of justice than are typical families today" (183). She concludes that the genderless family is more just for three reasons. First, it is more just to women. Second, it is more conducive to equal opportunity for women and children of both sexes, and, third, it creates a more favorable environment for rearing children in a just society. Her conclusion is that, if gender roles do disappear, then the family will be a much better place in which to develop a sense of justice.

CRITICISMS AND NEW DIRECTIONS

Okin's ideas on justice in the family have received a number of criticisms. In the following section, we will focus on two particularly pressing difficulties of her proposals. First, there is an unresolved tension within Okin's theory between freedom and justice. While Okin proposes that a completely just family is a "genderless" one, many people in free and pluralistic societies are unlikely to choose these kinds of families. Instead, many women and men will choose to live in traditional "gendered" families in which women perform most of the domestic labor. Okin herself recognizes that women who choose to devote themselves exclusively to parenting and homemaking will be protected in a society that is based on her principles of justice, and she also acknowledges that the "just society would include institutions that are acceptable to people who believe in the traditional divisions of labor between men and women" (180). It is clear that Okin must accept these unjust family arrangements as long as she accepts the freedom of association and the freedom of religion. However, Okin also argues that traditionally gendered families undermine the sound moral development of children. She holds that, unless the relationship between parents is just and "genderless," children "are likely to be considerably hindered in becoming people who are guided by principles of justice" (17).

If Okin is correct in her claims about the moral development of children, and if she is correct that a genderless family is a necessary condition for the development of mature and morally competent people, then it seems to follow that traditional families will be unacceptable within her just society. If traditional families are the breeding ground for injustice and inequality, then they ought not to be permitted. But, there is clearly a tension between her liberal commitment to respecting individuals' choices about how to arrange their family lives (a commitment that demands a relinquishing of the requirements of justice) and her commitment to justice as a primary good (a commitment that implies severely restricting people's choices in their personal lives). These aspects of her theory seem incompatible, and as it stands, both interpretations of her theory are unsatisfactory.

A second difficulty with Okin's theory has been described by Michael Sandel. In *Liberalism and the Limits of Justice*, Sandel points out that a Rawlsian conception of justice, which forms the background for Okin's theory of justice, applies primarily to societies and associations that understand themselves as a group of people with distinctive life plans and different conceptions of the good. It does not apply, in other words, to those engaged in joint ventures, in such associations as a family. Rawls writes in this context that

> . . . the circumstances of justice obtain whenever mutually disinterested persons put forward conflicting claims to the division of social advantages under conditions of moderate scarcity. Unless these circumstances existed there would be no occasion for the virtue of justice. . .[9]

Rawls' statement implies that associations or groups that share a common conception of the good, and that have strong bonds of love and mutual benevolence, are not subject to the circumstances of justice, and, thus, do not stand in need of principles of justice. Sandel suggests, in fact, that the enforcement of justice in these situations can lead to an overall moral decline in the quality of life. Sandel considers the example of close personal friendships. He writes:

> If, out of a misplaced sense of justice, a close friend of long-standing repeatedly insists on calculating and paying his precise share of every common expenditure, or refuses to accept any favor or hospitality ex-cept at the greatest protest and embarrassment, not only will I feel compelled to be reciprocally scrupulous but at some point may begin to wonder whether I have not misunderstood our relationship. The benevolence in our friendship will have diminished to the extent that the justice of our relationship has grown.[10]

Sandel concludes that justice is not always a virtue, and can even be a vice. This would hold especially true in associations where the members share common identities and purposes, such as a group of friends or a family. "In the institution of the family," Sandel writes, "affections

---

9. Rawls, John: *A Theory of Justice.* p. 128.
10. Sandel, Michael: *Liberalism and the Limits of Justice.* 1982, p. 35.

may be enlarged to such an extent that justice is scarcely engaged, much less as the 'first virtue.'"[11] Sandel's analysis of the role of justice in families raises an important objection to Okin's theory of justice in families. If Sandel is right, any family that gives first priority to justice encourages its members to see themselves as independent moral agents who are in potential conflict with each other regarding the distribution of assets and burdens. Okin's view of the family seems to overlook the fact that members of happy families pursue a common good. In fact, in many families it is nearly impossible to distinguish the interests of one member from those of another. This is especially true in the case of families with children. It is clear that children require tremendous sacrifices and investments, but (good) parents tend to view these sacrifices as being in their own interest, for they take their children's interests to be harmonious with or identical to their own. These considerations suggest that Okin puts too much emphasis on justice and, thus, fails to see that other virtues like benevolence, love, and, compassion are significantly more important for achieving a happy and well-functioning family than justice is.

These criticisms suggest that Okin does not have the last word on how to create just families. However, her ideas have been important in showing that the family is a potential source of exploitation, and have provided contemporary Anglo-American political philosophers with a reason to stop ignoring the family and instead define its role in a comprehensive theory of justice. In this regard, her work is of significant importance and will have lasting influence in Western political theory.

REFERENCES

Anderson, E., (1990). "Is women's labor a commodity?" *Philosophy and Public Affairs, 19*:1, 71–92.

Becker, G., (1981). A treatise on the family. Cambridge, MA: Harvard University Press.

Coontz, S., (1992). The way we never were: American families and the nostalgia trap. New York: Basic Books.

Dworkin, R., (1993). Life's dominion. New York: Vintage.

Firestone, S., (1970) The dialectics of sex: The case for feminist revolution. New York: William Morrow.

---

11. Ibid. p.169.

Folbre, N., (1994). Who pays for the kids? Gender and the structures of constraint. New York: Routledge.

Hampton, J., (1980). Contracts and choices: Does Rawls have a social contract theory?" *Journal of Philosophy*, JE *80;* 77: 315–338.

Gilligan, C., (1982). In a different voice: Psychological theory and women's development. Cambridge, MA: Harvard University Press.

Methods, Baltimore: Johns Hopkins University Press.

Hochschild, A., (1989). The second shift: Working parents and the revolution at home. New York: Viking Press.

MacKinnon, C., (1989). Toward a feminist theory of the state. Cambridge, MA: Harvard University Press.

Mill, J. S., (1869). The subjection of women. Indianapolis: Hackett, Publishing Co., 1988.

Nussbaum, M., (2000). Women and human development: The capabilities approach. Cambridge, MA: Cambridge University Press.

Okin, S., (1989). Justice, gender and the family. New York: Basic Books.

Pateman, C., (1983). Defending prostitution: Charges against Ericson. *Ethics 93*, 561–565.

Radin, M. J., (1988). Market inalienability. *Harvard Law Review, 100*, 1849–1937.

Rhode, D., (1997). Speaking of sex: The denial of gender inequality. Cambridge, MA: Harvard University Press.

-----. (1989). Justice and gender. Cambridge, MA: Harvard University Press.

Rich, A., (1976). Of woman born: Motherhood as experience and as institution. New York: Norton.

Rousseau, J. J., (1979). Emile: Or, on education. trans. A. Bloom, New York: Basic Books.

Sandel, M., (1982). Liberalism and the limits of justice. Cambridge, MA: Cambridge University Press.

Satz, D., (2003). Feminist perspectives on reproduction and the family. *The Stanford Encyclopedia of Philosophy (Winter 2004 Edition)*, Edward N. Zalta (ed.), URL http://plato.stanford.edu/archives/win2004 /entries/feminism-family/.

Chapter 7

THE EVOLUTION OF PSYCHOLOGISTS' RECOMMENDED CHILDREARING PRACTICES IN THE UNITED STATES

Michael J. Root

For centuries, parents in the United States (U.S.) have sought advice from various "experts" on how to effectively raise their children (e.g., Calvert, 2003; Geboy, 1981; Hulbert, 2003; Sather, 1989). In response, experts provided parents with guidance on myriad topics germane to raising children such as appropriate disciplinary practices, proper education and nutrition, regulating infant and child emotions, and the construction of safe physical environments. Expert advice came from individuals working in numerous fields including medicine, religion, philosophy, and psychology. Each generation's experts offered different types of advice reflecting their theoretical orientations in addition to the changing values and traditions in American society.

This chapter outlines the kinds of childrearing advice psychologists provided to parents in the U.S. from the time psychology emerged as an academic discipline to just after World War II (1880–1950). This seventy-year span was crucial for the discipline because psychologists' activities throughout this period helped establish psychology as a viable science (Morawski, 1988). Psychologists' childrearing advice to parents aided in this process because the research it generated demonstrated psychology's scientific nature and assisted in improving psychology's public image. A brief introduction to prepsychological thought on childrearing is provided to contextualize for the appearance of psychologists as advice givers. Following this, psychologists G. Stanley Hall, John B. Watson, Arnold L. Gesell, and B. F. Skinner, as representatives of the kinds of childrearing advice psychologists provided between 1880 and 1950, are discussed. Hall, Watson, and Gesell were successful in generating interest among parents for years. Skinner's childrearing strategy, on the other hand, met with parental resistance almost from the start. The chapter concludes with comments on the impact of psychologists' childrearing advice to parents building on this seventy-year period to present day.

PRE-PSYCHOLOGICAL THOUGHT ON CHILDREARING

There were no scientific studies of children in the seventeenth century. Most parents simply viewed children as miniature adults (van Drunen & Jansz, 2004). It was common at the time for parents in the U.S. to rely on Calvinist and Protestant ministers as experts on raising children. Ministers dispensed childrearing advice to parents in their sermons and books centered around the idea of original sin (Abramovitz, 1976). Children were born evil and it was only through hard work that they would find salvation. These ministers encouraged parents to demand strict obedience from their children and advocated instilling in them a strong work ethic in order to ensure the development of morally secure and virtuous adults.

By the eighteenth century, medical practitioners and philosophers started challenging the expertise of ministers. For example, medical practitioner James Parkinson, of Parkinson's disease fame, urged parents to raise their children in a kind and gentle manner (Pearn & Gardner-Thorpe, 2001). Similarly, philosophers John Locke and Jean-Jacques Rousseau espoused changing the ways parents educated and raised their children. Both Locke, who wrote the influential *Some Thoughts Concerning Education* (1693), and Rousseau, who published the widely popular *Émile, or on Education* (1763), believed that children developed *into* adults through their experiences in the world. Moreover, both philosophers stressed the importance of education and a nurturing family environment for healthy child development.

Parents began shifting their attention away from the harsh treatment and punishing discipline advocated by religious authorities and gravitated toward these other professions for childrearing advice. The idea of nurturing children promoted by many medical professionals and philosophers of the day implied that parents could play a significant role in shaping their children's futures. By following the advice of these experts, children could now be "made" into healthy, productive, and socially responsible adults.

The concept of "childhood" began acquiring its own developmental period due, in part, to a shift from the decidedly deterministic perspective of original sin to a perspective oriented more toward freedom of choice. Parents began perceiving children as children rather than as miniature adults. By the nineteenth century, childhood was firmly entrenched as a distinct period of human development that was qualitatively different from adulthood. This perspective change opened the door for scientists to begin studying the characteristics of childhood. Studies of their own children by the naturalist Charles Darwin (1877) and the French sociologist Hippolyte Taine (1877) exemplified this trend.

THE GENESIS OF PSYCHOLOGICAL THOUGHT ON CHILDREARING

The transition between the nineteenth and twentieth centuries in the U.S. was a time of rapid social transformation. The country's population changed from groups of relatively rural, agricultural villages to urban communities and industrialized cities. As U.S. cities grew in complexity, a pressing need for social management developed (van Drunen & Jansz, 2004). The implementation of social policies affected children in no small measure (Beatty, Cahan, & Grant, 2006; Croake & Glover, 1977; Hulbert, 2003; van Drunen & Jansz, 2004). By the 1830s, various social agencies began providing child welfare services. The 1890s saw most states in the U.S. institute compulsory education laws for children. Mothers, eager to find effective methods of raising children, formed the National Congress of Mothers in 1897. In the early 1900s, Congress instituted the Children's Bureau, which began publishing a popular childrearing advice pamphlet entitled *Infant Care.* Additionally, Congress took steps toward abolishing child labor.

It is within this social context that psychologists entered the forum for childrearing advice. Psychologists brought an array of theories, experimental methods, and technologies to this issue. Furthermore, psychologists took advantage of popular magazines such as *Parents' Magazine, Ladies' Home Journal,* and *Cosmopolitan* to disseminate their ideas on childrearing. These theories, methods, and technologies, accompanied by psychologists' writings in popular magazines, assisted in persuading parents to consider adopting psychologists' childrearing strategies.

Psychologists in the U.S. faced two challenges as they attempted to separate their discipline from departments of philosophy in colleges and universities in the late nineteenth century. First, they needed to establish credibility within academe by identifying subject matter that could be studied with the scientific rigor and experimental techniques used by established sciences such as physics and chemistry (Camfield, 1973). Second, they needed to promote the utility of psychological knowledge to a public who often mistook psychologists for psychics, palm readers, and spiritualists (Benjamin, 1986; Coon, 1992). It was G. Stanley Hall, the U.S.'s first Ph.D. in psychology, who believed that studying children could meet these two challenges. Hall assumed that psychologists could empirically test various dimensions of children's cognitive, behavioral, and affective abilities while, at the same time, publicize their findings about children's development to an eagerly awaiting public.

G. STANLEY HALL (1844–1924)

Granville Stanley Hall received his Ph.D. from Harvard University in 1878 under the tutelage of William James (Fancher, 1996). After obtaining his doctorate, he first worked as a lecturer and later a professor of psychology at Johns Hopkins University where he established one of the first psychological laboratories in America. Hall founded one of the first psychological journals, the *American Journal of Psychology,* in 1887, and helped form the American Psychological Association in 1892. In 1888, he accepted the post of university president at the newly formed Clark University.

Hall's theory on children's development derived from his Puritan upbringing and evolutionary theory. He believed in the now discredited theory of recapitulation, which permeated much of his published work (Noon, 2005). Developed by zoologist Ernst Haeckel in 1866, recapitulation theory proposed that, as individuals progressed through developmental stages, they mimicked the stages seen in the development of humans as a species, i.e., ontogeny recapitulates phylogeny (Bowler, 1989). As such, Hall's developmental theory was deterministic. Children go through specific, unchangeable stages of physical, emotional, and mental development on their way to adulthood. Hall's recapitulationist ideas led to his belief that the role of parents in raising children should be one of providing children with as much love and attention as possible in order to facilitate healthy development.

It was at Clark University that Hall began his studies of children and childrearing, specifically in relation to education. Describing the importance of studying child education, Hall (1903) stated: "It is doing a work for the child at school akin to that of the Reformation for the religious life of adults" (p. 97). Beginning in 1883, Hall and his students at Clark administered thousands of questionnaires to educators and parents around the country in order to gain insight into the way children learn and develop. Hall's studies were the beginning of the child study movement in America and, because of his efforts, he is often credited as being the "father" of child psychology (e.g., Elkind, 1992; McCullers, 1969). The questionnaires Hall and his students sent to educators and parents focused on numerous topics such as "fears in childhood and youth," "dreams," "crying and laughing," "the relation of the school and home," and "the study of punishment" (White, 1990). Using the questionnaire data, Hall began disseminating childrearing advice in public lectures and in publications. Hall published many of his findings in popular magazines such as *Ladies' Home Journal* and *Appleton's Magazine* to appeal to as many parents as possible. His advice for parents covered an array of topics including the dangers of premature exercise in motor development, the harm of rote rehearsal in learning, and the physical confinement of grade-school children (Cahan, 2006). As parents and educators responded to these questionnaires, attended his lectures, and read his publications, Hall's reputation as a childrearing expert grew. The National Congress of Mothers, for instance, was impressed enough with Hall's questionnaire research that it adopted him as one of its spokespeople.

Based on data obtained from these questionnaires, Hall published his two-volume seminal treatise, *Adolescence*, in 1904. This publication helped situate adolescence as a distinct developmental stage between childhood and adulthood. The historian Hamilton Cravens (2006) has suggested that this book "helped import science and scholarship into the traditional discourses on . . . adolescence" (p. 172). *Adolescence* sold over 25,000 copies in its first printing (Cahan, 2006). Interestingly, it was parents wanting information on a new developmental stage, not psychologists, who made most of the purchases. According to Lorine Pruette, Hall's first biographer, "mothers . . . hugged its two big volumes to their breasts . . . [finding] . . . within its thousand pages a light to ease their steps and to guide them through the perilous paths of childrearing" (as cited in Hulbert, 2003, p. 60). At the time, parents found Hall's advice about childhood and adolescence in line with their beliefs that children needed nurturing instead of discipline in the home (Brooks-Gunn & Johnson, 2006).

While Hall enjoyed a successful relationship with parents throughout the child study movement, psychologists began scrutinizing his research. Many psychologists, such as E. L. Thorndike, criticized Hall's research as solely descriptive rather than experimental (Brooks-Gunn & Johnson, 2006). Another complaint from Hall's critics was that his deterministic theories left little room for parents and educators in shaping their children's futures. The role of parents was to create enough of a nurturing environment for children to develop in an already predetermined manner. By the 1920s, parents and educators who realized the implications of Hall's deterministic perspective began searching for other psychological experts to help them raise their children. Many parents in the 1920s turned to the behaviorist, John Watson, for assistance.

JOHN B. WATSON (1878–1958)

John Broadus Watson received his Ph.D. from the University of Chicago in 1903 under the training of James Rowland Angell (Harris, 1999b). The department of psychology and philosophy at Johns Hopkins University hired Watson in 1908 and he became the head of the department the following year. He began an affair with his graduate assistant, Rosalie Rayner, and when the affair became public in 1920, Watson resigned from Johns Hopkins and began working at the J. Walter Thompson advertising agency in New York. It was during the mid-to-late 1920s that Watson started publishing popular advice about childrearing.

While at Johns Hopkins, Watson published two seminal papers that played a significant role in the kind of advice he presented to parents. First was his (1913) theoretical vision of behaviorism, which was a radical departure from the traditional introspective methods used by most psychologists at the time. In the paper, Watson proposed that psychologists base their science on empirical observations of behavior rather than subjective reports of internal mental processes. Watson's (1920) second paper was a report of the famous "Little Albert" experiment, which he carried out with Rayner. Watson (1917) believed that infants were born with three basic emotions: fear, rage, and love. His understanding of classical conditioning led him to believe that repeated pairings of a stimulus eliciting one of the innate emotions and a stimulus that elicited no emotion, would eventually lead to an emotional reaction to the stimulus that originally elicited no emotion. In the study, Watson and Rayner attempted to classically condition a fear response to a neutral stimulus (e.g., a white rat) in Albert by banging a claw hammer and metal bar behind Albert's head while presenting him with a white rat. While Albert's fear response to the rat was transitory, the study reinforced Watson's belief that the use of classical conditioning could change people's behavior.

Watson's childrearing advice appeared in many magazines for the lay public including *McCall's, Cosmopolitan, The Nation, Liberty,* and *Harper's Monthly* (Harris, 1984). What is apparent from these popular advice articles is the contrast between Watson's and Hall's approaches. Hall's approach was unquestionably deterministic. Conversely, Watson approached childrearing from an environmentalist position. For example, in an article for *Harper's* magazine, Watson (1926) claimed that his behaviorist ideas could "build any man, starting at birth, into any kind of social or asocial being upon order" (p. 728). He believed parents' behavior toward their children played a significant role in child development. Coddling children, especially by mothers, would lead to the breakdown of society by producing a population of weak-minded adults. His position was that parents needed to take a "hands off" approach concerning displays of affection to prevent spoiling the child. However, he did propose rigid guidelines and schedules for parents to follow in raising their children.

In 1928, Watson published his magnum opus on childrearing, *Psychological Care of Infant and Child.* An advertisement for *Psychological Care* in *Ladies' Home Journal* (1930) described the book as "the standard work on child psychology." The same advertisement proclaimed Watson's book as "perhaps the most important book ever written" (p. 67). In the book, Watson continued advocating his rigid style of child-rearing. In one section, Watson directed parents to "Never hug and kiss [their children], never let them sit in your lap. If you must, kiss them once on the forehead when they say good night. Shake hands with them in the morning" (pp. 81–82). Parents eagerly purchased Watson's book, which became a bestseller. Parents found his advice appealing due to his practical suggestions. Watson gave parents advice on issues common to childrearing such as controlling children's temper tantrums, thumb sucking, and childhood fears.

Watson's childrearing advice remained popular with parents in the 1920s and throughout the decade of the Great Depression. During the 1940s, however, parents' attention shifted to two other experts on child-rearing: Benjamin Spock and Arnold Gesell. While the impact of Spock's childrearing manuals have been covered extensively (e.g., Graebner, 1980; Weiss, 1977), much less is known about Gesell's work.

ARNOLD L. GESELL (1880–1961)

In a 1961 editorial on Gesell's death from New Haven's *Register*, one individual remarked: "In countless American homes the name of Arnold L. Gesell was better known than that of the President of the United States. And to a great number of the occupants of those homes Arnold Gesell was a far more important man than the occupant of the White House" (as cited in Ames, 1961, p. 266). This quote personifies the public's feelings about Gesell and his contributions to childrearing. As parents grew tired of Watson's regimented childrearing schedules, they found appealing advice in Gesell's research.

Arnold Lucius Gesell received his doctorate in psychology in 1906 from Clark University under the direction of G. Stanley Hall (Harris, 1999a). As a student at Clark, Hall's child study movement inspired Gesell. He later received a medical degree at Yale University in 1915. While at Yale, he became the director of the Clinic of Child Development in addition to working part time for the Connecticut Board of Education (Benjamin & Baker, 2004).

Gesell combined Hall's deterministic vision of development with scientifically and technologically advanced methods of identifying children's developmental stages. Gesell (1946) advocated using film and photography in the laboratory to capture developmental milestones. He said of the importance of film in child research: "The cinema sees with an all-seeing, impartial eye and it records with an infallible memory. We need such a powerful recording instrument for the exploration of the bewildering . . . eventfulness of human infancy" (Gesell, 1932, p. 266). Additionally, Gesell created an observational dome in which to film, observe, and photograph children performing various developmental tasks. Gesell often distributed these films to the public, sometimes showing them in department stores (Hulbert, 2003). Parents became fascinated with motion pictures of children and entertained the possibility of watching their own children achieve developmental milestones.

Evidence of his impact on parents occurred in 1928 when *Parents' Magazine* awarded Gesell its prize for outstanding book in child psychology for *Infancy and Human Growth*, even beating out Watson's *Psychological Care of Infant and Child*. While most of Gesell's books were of a scientific nature, he tried to write for the lay public (Senn, 1975). In the 1940s, Gesell published two influential books on childrearing: *Infant and Child in the Culture of Today* (1943) and *The Child from Five to Ten* (1946). Both books became bestsellers. In the books, Gesell took a middle ground approach to childrearing between excessive permissiveness and strict discipline. Parents were attracted to Gesell's childrearing books because they presented parents with a look at the "normal" child. The books contained information pertaining to developmental timetables and milestones. By 1947, these developmental timetables were the most popular developmental measures in the country (Herman, 2001). Parents could now compare their own children's development with Gesell's prescribed milestones. Comparing their own children's development with the children from Gesell's laboratory at Yale appealed to parents because they could chart their own children's progress and adjust their parenting styles to accommodate the varying needs of their children.

While Gesell enjoyed success at providing parents with childrearing advice for several decades, parents did not respond as affectionately to attempts made by B. F. Skinner, arguably the most famous psychologist of the twentieth century. In fact, many parents in the 1940s and 1950s perceived Skinner's childrearing advice as cruel and inhumane.

B. F. SKINNER (1904–1990)

Burrhus Frederic Skinner received his Ph.D. from Harvard University in 1931 (Fancher, 1996). He worked at several universities throughout his career including Indiana University and the University of Minnesota. Skinner's reputation grew out of his development of operant conditioning and creation of the Skinner box. In operant conditioning, desired behaviors are increased by the introduction of a stimulus (e.g., reward or mild shock). The Skinner box was an apparatus that housed laboratory animals in which various stimuli were introduced to increase desired behaviors in the animals. For instance, Skinner could increase the number of times a laboratory rat pressed a lever by rewarding the rat with food pellets every time it pressed the lever. In his research, Skinner combined rigorous observations of behaviors with technological devices (Smith, 1992). As an example, during World War II he attempted to train pigeons using operant conditioning as missile guidance systems in a research project called "Project Pigeon" (Skinner, 1960).

In 1945, Skinner published an article in *Ladies' Home Journal* entitled "Baby in a Box" about an invention he developed for raising infants called the "baby tender." The baby tender was an enclosed, temperature controlled crib with a safety glass window in the front. The crib was fitted with a canvas bottom covered by a sheet on which to place the baby. Parents could observe their baby through the window. When the baby slept, parents could pull a curtain over the window to provide darkness.

The inspiration for the baby tender, also known as the "air crib," was Yvonne Skinner's (Skinner's wife) frustration with the daily routine of raising their first child (Skinner, 1945). Skinner went to work designing the baby tender as a means of increasing his wife's leisure time with their second daughter, Deborah. The Skinners raised Deborah in the baby tender for the first years of her life. In describing the effects of raising Deborah in the baby tender, Skinner reported that, unlike many children, his daughter slept comfortably, was free of any illnesses, and developed an admirable tolerance for annoyances.

The article prompted other magazines such as *Life* and *Time* to publish their own accounts of the baby tender. Because of these accounts, it did not take long for the baby tender to acquire public exposure. Skinner attempted to market the baby tender to the public and even went into business with an engineer, John Gray, to mass market the device (Benjamin & Nielsen-Gammon, 1999). Parents experimentally raising their own children in baby tenders reported satisfaction and positive outcomes with the device. In fact, Skinner reported that most of the letters he received regarding the baby tender were positive in nature.

The idea of raising children in the baby tender, however, bothered many parents. Parents had many issues with the baby tender including the lack of parent-child contact, the possibility of infant suffocation, the lack of social interactions, and the absence of experimental evidence on its efficacy (Benjamin & Nielsen-Gammon, 1999; Rutherford, 2003). Quite simply, parents had difficulty with the idea of raising their children in boxes. Parents viewed this childrearing strategy as cruel and inhumane. In the end, Skinner's technological creation never reached the level of public popularity as the ideas of Hall, Watson, and Gesell.

CONCLUSIONS

In the U.S., parents' perceptions of how to successfully raise their children have changed throughout the centuries. One of the reasons for this change is the expert advice they received from religious authorities, medical practitioners, philosophers, and psychologists. With the advent of the concept of "childhood," psychologists were able to begin investigating children's development. Based on their findings, psychologists began proposing childrearing strategies to parents.

Throughout the first half of the twentieth century, psychologists and parents developed a reciprocal relationship in their collaborative search to find effective childrearing practices. Parents called upon psychologists to provide them with definitive answers as to the proper care of their children. Psychologists, with varying degrees of success, answered the call by publishing books and popular magazine articles, lecturing to the public, and developing new technologies. As this trend continued from the 1880s to the 1950s, the public began viewing psychologists as experts on children's mental, behavioral, and emotional life.

In the 1960s, social and political changes dominated the American landscape. Due to psychologists' expert knowledge of children, policy makers began looking to them for guidance on social policies affecting children (Cahan, 2006). Projects in the 1960s such as the Head Start program, which focused on providing early childhood education to disadvantaged children, exemplify these policy changes. In response, psychologists began focusing more on the scientific dimensions of studying children to provide data for policy makers' decisions and less on popularized child rearing advice. As a result of this shift in focus, the sub-discipline of developmental psychology grew in popularity (White, 2003). The primary concern of developmental psychologists became studies of children's cognitive abilities, especially as these abilities pertained to education, instead of childrearing advice for parents. French psychologist Jean Piaget's theory of children's cognitive development, for example, became a central theme for U.S. psychologists studying children in the 1960s and 1970s. Additionally, Russian psychologist Lev Vygotsky's sociocultural theory of development became popular among developmental psychologists in the 1970s. Both Piaget's and Vygotsky's theories continue to influence developmental psychologists' perceptions and understanding of children.

As developmental psychologists continued to focus on the research dimension of their profession from the 1960s to the present, there was a change in the way parents received childrearing advice. Psychologists seemed less likely to engage with parents in the way they did in the first half of the twentieth century. In fact, little of psychologists' current research ever directly reaches parents via psychologists. Instead, professionals such as journalists and newscasters have taken over the responsibilities of transmitting psychologists' childrearing research to the public (Burnham, 1987). Currently, parents seeking childrearing advice have to rely on these professionals' interpretations of psychologists' research. It appears that the procedures used by psychologists such as Hall, Watson, Gesell, and Skinner to get their messages to parents are now out of fashion. Today, newspapers, magazines, and the Internet inundate parents with distilled, and sometimes inaccurate, versions of the most effective means of caring for, educating, and raising their children.

REFERENCES

Abramovitz, R. (1976). Parenthood in America. *Journal of Clinical and Child Psychology, 5*, 43–46.

Ames, L. B. (1961). Arnold L. Gesell: "Behavior has shape." *Science, 134*, 266–267.

Beatty, B., Cahan, E. D., & Grant, J. (Eds.). (2006). *When science encounters the child: Education, parenting, and child welfare in 20th century America.* New York: Teachers College Press.

Benjamin, L. T. (1986). Why don't they understand us? A history of psychology's public image. *American Psychologist, 41*, 941–946.

Benjamin, L. T., & Baker, D. B. (2004). *From séance to science: A history of the profession of psychology in America.* Belmont, CA: Wadsworth.

Benjamin, L. T., & Nielsen-Gammon, E. (1999). B. F. Skinner and psychotechnology: The case of the heir conditioner. *Review of General Psychology, 3*, 155–167.

Bowler, P. J. (1989). *Evolution: The history of an idea* (Rev. ed.). Berkeley, CA: University of California Press.

Brooks-Gunn, J., & Johnson, A. D. (2006). G. Stanley Hall's contribution to science, practice and policy: The child study, parent education, and child welfare movements. *History of Psychology, 9*, 247–258.

Burnham, J. C. (1987). *How superstition won and science lost: Popularizing science and health in the United States.* New Brunswick, NJ: Rutgers University Press.

Cahan, E. D. (2006). Toward a socially relevant science: Notes on the history of child development research. In B. Beatty, E. D. Cahan, & J. Grant (Eds.), *When science encounters the child: Education, parenting, and child welfare in 20th century America* (pp. 16–34). New York: Teachers College Press.

Calvert, K. (2003). Patterns of childrearing in America. In W. Koops & M. Zuckerman (Eds.), *Beyond the century of the child: Cultural history and developmental psychology* (pp. 62–81). Philadelphia: University of Pennsylvania Press.

Camfield, T. M. (1973). The professionalization of American psychology, 1870–1917. *Journal of the History of the Behavioral Sciences, 9*, 66–75.

Coon, D. J. (1992). Testing the limits of sense and science: American experimental psychologists combat spiritualism, 1880–1920. *American Psychologist, 47*, 143–151.

Cravens, H. (2006). The historical context of G. Stanley Hall's Adolescence (1904). *History of Psychology, 9*, 172–185.

Croake, J. W., & Glover, K. E. (1977). A history and evaluation of parent education. *The Family Coordinator, 26*, 151–158.

Darwin, C. (1877). A biographical sketch of an infant. *Mind, 2*, 285–294.

Elkind, D. (1992). Child development research. In S. Koch & D. E. Leary (Eds.), *A century of psychology as science* (pp. 472–488). Washington, DC: American Psychological Association.

Fancher, R. E. (1996). *Pioneers of psychology.* New York: Norton.

Geboy, M. J. (1981). Who is listening to the "experts"? The use of child care materials by parents. *Family Relations, 30*, 205–210.

Gesell, A. (1928). *Infancy and human growth.* New York: Macmillan.

Gesell, A. (1932). How science studies the child. *Scientific Monthly, 34*, 265–267.

Gesell, A. (1946). Cinematography and the study of child development. *The American Naturalist, 80,* 470–475.

Gesell, A., & Ilg, F. L. (1943). *Infant and child in the culture of today: The guidance of development in home and nursery school.* New York: Harper & Brothers.

Gesell, A., & Ilg, F. L. (1946). *The child from five to ten.* New York: Harper & Brothers.

Graebner, W. (1980). The unstable world of Benjamin Spock: Social engineering in a democratic culture, 1917-1950. *Journal of American History, 67,* 612–629.

Hall, G. S. (1903). Child study at Clark University: An impending new step. *American Journal of Psychology, 14,* 96–106.

Hall, G. S. (1904). *Adolescence: Its psychology and its relation to physiology, anthropology, sociology, sex, crime, religion and education.* New York: Appleton.

Harris, B. (1984). "Give me a dozen healthy infants . . . " In M. Lewin (Ed.), *In the shadow of the past: Psychology portrays the sexes* (pp. 126–154). New York: Columbia University Press.

Harris, B. (1999a). Arnold Gesell. In J. A. Garraty & M. C. Carnes (Eds.), *American National Biography* (pp. 877–878). New York: Oxford University Press.

Harris, B. (1999b). John Broadus Watson. In J. A. Garraty & M. C. Carnes (Eds.), *American National Biography* (pp. 795–797). New York: Oxford University Press.

Herman, E. (2001). Families made by science: Arnold Gesell and the technologies of modern child adoption. *Isis, 92,* 684–715.

Hulbert, A. (2003). *Raising America: Experts, parents, and a century of advice about children.* New York: Alfred A. Knopf.

Locke, J. (1693). *Some thoughts concerning education.* London: Churchill.

McCullers, J. C. (1969). G. Stanley Hall's conception of mental development and some indications of its influence on developmental psychology. *American Psychologist, 24,* 1109–1114.

Morawski, J. (Ed.). (1988). *The rise of experimentation in American psychology.* New Haven, CT: Yale University Press.

Noon, D. H. (2005). The evolution of beasts and babies: Recapitulation, instinct, and the early discourse on child development. *Journal of the History of the Behavioral Sciences, 41,* 367–386.

Pearn, J., & Gardner-Thorpe, C. (2001). James Parkinson (1977–1824): A pioneer of child care. *Journal of Paediatric Child Health, 37,* 9–13.

Rousseau. (1763). *Émile, or on education.* London: Nousse and Vaillant.

Rutherford, A. (2003). B. F. Skinner's technology of behavior in American life: From consumer culture to counterculture. *Journal of the History of the Behavioral Sciences, 39,* 1–23.

Sather, K. (1989). Sixteenth and seventeenth century child-rearing: A matter of discipline. *Journal of Social History, 22,* 735–743.

Senn, M., J. E. (1975). Insights on the child development movement in the United States. *Monographs for the Society for Research in Child Development, 40*(3/4), 1–107.

Skinner, B. F. (1945). Baby in a box. *Ladies' Home Journal, October,* 30–31, 135–136, 138.

Skinner, B. F. (1960). Pigeons in a pelican. *American Psychologist, 15,* 28–37.

Smith, L. D. (1992). On prediction and control: B. F. Skinner and the technological ideal of science. *American Psychologist, 47,* 216–223.

Taine, H. (1877). M. Taine on the acquisition of language by children. *Mind, 2,* 252–259.

van Drunen, P., & Jansz, J. (2004). Child-rearing and education. In J. Jansz & P. van Drunen (Eds.), *A social history of psychology* (pp. 45–92). Malden, MA: Blackwell.

Watson, J. B. (1913). Psychology as the behaviorist views it. *Psychological Review, 20,* 158–177.

Watson, J. B. (1926). What is behaviorism? *Harper's Magazine, 152,* 723–729.

Watson, J. B., & Morgan, J. J. B. (1917). Emotional reactons and psychological experimentation. *American Journal of Psychology, 28,* 163–174.

Watson, J. B., & Rayner, R. (1920). Conditioned emotional reactions. *Journal of Experimental Psychology, 10,* 421–428.

Watson, J. B. (1930). I am the mother of a behaviorist's son. *Parent's Magazine, December,* 16–18, 67.

Weiss, N. P. (1977). Mother, the invention of necessity: Dr. Benjamin Spock's baby and child care. *American Quarterly, 29,* 519–546.

White, S. H. (1990). Child study at Clark University: 1894–1904. *Journal of the History of the Behavioral Sciences, 26,* 131–150.

White, S. H. (2003). Developmental psychology in a world of designed institutions. In W. Koops & M. Zuckerman (Eds.), *Beyond the century of the child: Cultural history and developmental psychology* (pp. 204–223). Philadelphia: University of Pennsylvania Press.

Chapter 8

THE INFLUENCE OF SOCIAL SUPPORT IN THE FAMILY ON THE HEALTH OF FAMILY MEMBERS

Monair J. Hamilton

Empirical evidence confirms the influence of parents, caretakers, and adults deemed significant in the lives of children and adolescents on improved academic outcomes in school as well as on the long-term health behaviors of youth (Telljohann, Symons, & Pateman, 2007). Research also indicates "Positive attitudes toward health behavior are more likely to lead to higher levels of readiness to engage in activity, self-efficacious judgments of one's ability to engage in positive health behavior, and acquisition of higher levels of disease risk awareness" (Walcott-McQuigg, Zerwic, Dan, & Kelley, 2001, p. 8). Positive attitudes are particularly important as health behaviors in childhood and adolescence can translate into lifelong health-enhancing behaviors; positive attitudes will encourage adolescents to engage in physical activity. Reinforcing this theme, Trost et al. (1997) asserted:

> Observation of a significant relationship between self-efficacy in overcoming barriers and future physical activity behavior among elementary school children is particularly noteworthy. This suggests that parents, teachers, other significant adults, and, where possible, peers should assist low-active children in overcoming traditional barriers to physical activity such as time constraints, homework obligations, and feelings of fatigue. (p. 261)

It is in this context that the focus on health within the family structure will be discussed. Physical activity is one element among numerous indicators that contributes to individual health status. Adolescents face challenges in overcoming barriers of psychosocial influences over physical activity. Dismissing these elements is not the best strategy in helping them make positive strides toward a healthier lifestyle.

HEALTH STATUS OF AMERICANS

American's public health agenda for the next decade was defined with the publication of *Healthy People 2010: Understanding and Improving Health* (USDHHS, 2000). As part of this national strategy, baseline data were provided and objectives specified for promoting health, reducing preventable death and disability, and enhancing the quality of life for all. Public health professionals were charged with the responsibility of focusing their energies on confronting the challenge of two overarching goals:

1. Increase quality and years of healthy life, and
2. Eliminate health disparities (USDHHS, 2000).

Healthy People 2010 described 10 leading health indicators that reflect the major public health priorities in the United States. These indicators included physical activity, overweight and obesity, tobacco use, substance abuse, responsible sexual behavior, mental health, injury and violence, environmental quality, immunization, and access to health care (USDHHS, 2000). In addition to these identified indicators, research has determined that there are multiple levels of influence that contribute to the health status and quality of life of all Americans. These influences can originate with individual behaviors, physical and social environmental factors, or access to quality health care (USDHHS, 2000). Health status can be quantified in the context of morbidity and mortality rates or quality of life indicators.

In related research, McGinnis and Foege (1993) investigated morbidity and mortality by contrasting the clinical diagnosis of patients at the time of death with the root cause of their death. This examination of the "actual causes of death" of individuals in the United States identified the contributions of various nongenetic factors to premature morbidity and mortality. In addition, nongenetic factors were determined to be related to diminished quality of life. These nongenetic factors included tobacco use, diet and activity patterns, alcohol, infectious agents, toxic agents, firearms, sexual behavior, motor vehicles, illicit use of drugs, and other factors (McGinnis & Foege). Importantly, the investigation reinforced the contribution of individual behaviors to premature death and disability among Americans.

In a follow-up study, Mokdad, Marks, Stroup, and Gerberding (2004) re-examined the work of McGinnis and Foege (1993) and compiled current epidemiological, clinical, and laboratory studies with a particular focus on the contribution of various factors to U.S. mortality. This update revealed that close to half of all deaths among Americans result from preventable behaviors and exposures to unhealthful substances (Mokdad et al., 2004). Moreover, this analysis revealed one important change not in evidence at the time of the earlier work conducted by McGinnis and Foege (1993). Specifically, although McGinnis and Foege estimated that 300,000 deaths per year were caused by poor diets and physical inactivity, Mokdad et al. estimated that 400,000 deaths are attributable to these particular behaviors. This represents a significant increase of deaths specifically related to diet and inactivity and is the largest increase among all actual causes of death (Mokdad et al.). Although specific analytical approaches differed between the work of McGinnis and Foege and that of Mokdad et al., it was concluded that poor diet and physical inactivity, along with alcohol and tobacco use, account for a substantial proportion of preventable deaths in the United States (Mokdad et al.).

The calculations in the findings published by Mokdad et al. (2005) were recently corrected in the *Journal of the American Medical Association.* Mokdad et al. (2004) originally estimated that 400,000 deaths were attributable to poor diets and physical inactivity, an increase of 100,000 from the previous estimate of McGinnis and Foege (1993). The corrected calculation adjusts the approximate increase to 65,000 from such specific behaviors instead of the published increase of 100,000 deaths. Statistically, the adjustment accounts for 15.2 percent of deaths attributed to poor diets and physical inactivity instead of 16 percent (Mokdad et al., 2005). Although the conclusion remains unchanged, that poor diet and physical inactivity account for a substantial proportion of preventable deaths in the United States, it was important to clarify the potential double-count of deaths attributed to these specific behaviors (Mokdad et al., 2005).

PHYSICAL ACTIVITY AMONG ADOLESCENTS

Research confirms that the number of overweight Americans has increased across all segments of the population (USDHHS, 2000, 2004; USDHHS & USDA, 2005). The effects of being overweight manifest themselves years after an individual experiences initial excessive weight gain. Such is the case surrounding childhood and adolescent obesity. Benefits of regular physical activity in adolescents can include weight management and control, decreased blood pressure, and improved cardio-respiratory health. In addition, MacKay, Fingerhut, and Duran (2000) asserted that individuals who begin participating in a physically active lifestyle during adolescence are more likely to continue this behavior pattern through adulthood. Literature in health education confirms that behaviors affecting all areas of a person's character and personality are cultivated during childhood and follow the individual through adulthood (MacKay et al., 2000; Melnyk & Weinstein, 1994; USDHHS, 2000). Physical activity in childhood and adolescence can shape health status throughout an individual's natural life. Longitudinal studies have demonstrated "the importance of an active lifestyle for promoting health and wellbeing" (Leonard, 2001, p. 161). The main problem for the health educator, or any individual for that matter, in this instance is to understand how to "promote a fit and active lifestyle earlier in life so as to reduce chronic disease risks later in life" (p. 159).

Disabling conditions resulting from being overweight and obese are not limited to adults; extending the benefits for chronic disease reduction to adolescents becomes increasingly important as they can manifest disabling conditions earlier in life. According to MacKay et al. (2000), physical inactivity can lead to a number of negative health outcomes for adolescents. Such concerns include Type-2 diabetes, high blood lipids, hypertension, malnutrition, and orthopedic problems. In reviewing the School Health Policies and Programs Study conducted in 2000, the prevalence of overweight children aged six to eleven years in the United States had nearly doubled from 7 percent in the years ranging 1976–1980, to 13 percent in 1999. The prevalence of overweight adolescents aged twelve to nineteen years in the United States increased from 5 percent in 1976–1980 to 14 percent in 1999 (Wechsler, Brener, Kuester, & Miller, 2001). This is a serious concern, particularly among children who show evidence of the early onset of common chronic illnesses that normally would not be manifested until adulthood. In recent years, increasing numbers of children are at higher risk for all chronic diseases including premature heart disease due, in part, to their dietary habits. Such risks are reinforced by data confirming that the average total fat and saturated fat content of school breakfasts and lunches exceed targets recommended in the Dietary Guidelines for Americans (USDHHS, 2005; Wechsler et al., 2001).

The difficulty in addressing physical inactivity or sedentary lifestyles among Americans, specifically highlighting young people, is reflected in the lack of importance placed on physical activity in schools. *Healthy People* 2010 discusses the association between the developmental stages and the lack of physical activity noting "participation in all types of physical activity declines strikingly as age or grade in school increases . . . [and] adolescents' interest and participation in physical activity differ by gender" (USDHHS, 2000, pp. 22–4, 22–5). In the early 1990s, Covey and Feltz (1991) studied patterns of physical activity among adolescents. A major finding was that many adolescent high school girls self-reported on the instrument as being physically active. It was believed at the time that either it was socially desirable to be physically active or at least socially desirable to report being physically active on the survey in high school. Those high school girls identifying themselves as reporting a decreased physical activity level also reported this decrease as due to a "lack of time and the demands of other important activities in their lives, such as jobs, schoolwork, chores, etc." (Covey & Feltz, p. 472). This psychosocial influence over physical activity reflected that, even as early as adolescence, these girls have to make hard choices between activities that are seemingly more important, such as homework and other responsibilities, and are not focusing on opportunities to participate in physical activity.

Current literature, however, suggests that many adolescents do participate in physical activity. Researchers have found that "over two-thirds (70 percent) of all high school students participate in moderate to vigorous physical activity . . . but female and male students in grade nine were more likely to have participated in moderate or vigorous physical activity than students in grades ten to twelve (MacKay et al., 2000, p. 84). This reflects that, as many adolescents increase in age, their interest in physical activity declines. Participation in physical activity also differs by sex, as male students are more likely than female students to participate in moderate or vigorous physical activity (MacKay et al.).

FAMILY INFLUENCE ON HEALTH

Elementary and secondary schools are uniquely positioned to improve the health of children and adolescents with over 95 percent of students enrolled in educational institutions nationwide each school day (Kolbe, Kann, Patterson, Wechsler, Osorio, & Collins, 2004). Schools are a natural fit for health information dissemination, but cannot be expected to take sole responsibility for addressing the needs of youth; parental involvement is ideal. The education level of parents has been found to influence the overall health as well as physical activity participation levels among their children. Importantly, the influence of this variable differs according to race. Research suggests that, "as white girls get older, physical activity may become more self-motivated and less influenced by parents. In contrast for black girls, an inverse association between parental education and decline in activity was manifested only at older ages" (Kimm et al., 2002, p. 713). The education level among black women has an effect on their levels of physical activity. Researchers asserted:

> Having 12 or more years of education and knowledge of the number of days per week needed for exercise to strengthen the heart were the only factors associated with a change from inactive to active status in the longitudinal follow-up. (Adam-Campbell et al., 2000, p. 47)

Familial influence on the overall health and physical activity participation levels of children is not limited to education. The self-image of children can be significantly affected by parents, caregivers, and other family members. Immediate family members such as mother/grandmother, sister/brother influenced the body size of black participants in a study focused on body image. Black females were influenced by family members, as well as authority figures with which those black females were in regular contact, such as teachers and administrators. "These results suggest black adolescents are influenced more by adult role models in terms of body size preference development" (Parnell et al., 1996, p. 117). This information reinforces that, to "successfully reach black female adolescents, role models from their families and community must be identified. This can be a challenge, as the culture of obesity tolerance may provide mostly role models who themselves are overweight or obese" (Melnyk & Weinstein, 1994, p. 539).

The theme of attractiveness through parental acceptance and rejection carries over to African American girls. In a report from the

National Heart, Lung, and Blood Institute Growth and Health Study, nine- and ten-year-old black girls reported feeling accepted in social situations regardless of their degree of adiposity, while white girls with greater adiposity felt rejected (Kimm et al., 2002). It has been documented that the levels of physical activity decline during adolescence in the United States, and especially among girls. This seems to begin in early adolescence, but "its rate accelerated so that by the ages of 18–19 years, the majority of the girls engaged in virtually no habitual physical activities other than those performed during school" (Kimm et al., p. 712).

SOCIAL SUPPORT

It is in this context of recognizing the powerful influence of familial relationships on the overall health of adolescents and children that the theoretical constructs of social support can be applied. Empirical evidence suggests that membership in a support system or network can increase participation in physical activity. Social support has several domains, constructs, and definitions. The concept of social support has been defined as:

> Interpersonal transactions that include one or more of the following: affect (expressions of liking, loving, admiration, respect), affirmation (expressions of agreement or acknowledgement of the appropriateness or rightness of some act, statement or point of view), and aid (transactions in which direct aid or assistance is given, including things, money, information, advice, time or entitlement). (Kahn & Antonucci, as cited in Sarason, Sarason, & Pierce, 1990a, p. 175)

There is considerable variation of the social support concept in research, which has resulted in numerous forms of measurement and application. Social support is known as a primary influence on health as individuals in socially supportive environments function best.

This theory is deeply ingrained in the interpersonal level of interaction and is referred to as a contract of either "mothering" or "smothering" an individual (Sarason et al., 1990b). Social support is also highly subjective to the individual, for if the recipient does not perceive the support to be available, the support being given might not be helpful, or even utilized. Also, the sender of the support might not be viewed as being helpful by the recipient or the type of support being given might not meet the needs of the recipient (Sarason et al., 1990b). Understanding these basic concepts of the social support theory leads to a better understanding of its core constructs, "social support (a) contributes to positive adjustment and personal development and (b) provides a buffer against the effects of stress" (Sarason et al., 1983, p. 127).

Over the years, several studies have linked social support and physical activity participation. The purpose of one such study, in 1987, was to assist in the development of measures for social support for exercise behaviors (Sallis et al., 1987). Previous studies suggested that "social support was an important determinant of health-behavior change" (Sallis et al., p. 833). The participants of the study were all forty-five years old or younger, had children in the household, and were to be in the process of changing their exercise patterns. The social support scale that was used had the participants rate the frequency with which their "family and friends had said or done what was described in the item during the previous 3 months" (Sallis et al., p. 833). Findings included that "family involvement in exercise was more extensive than friend involvement" (Sallis et al., p. 833). Researchers suggested that many health interventions improve social support and that the development of social support scales can be an effective measure in assessing these heath-promotion interventions (Sallis et al.).

SOCIAL SUPPORT FROM FAMILY SOURCES

A review of the current literature reveals that there is evidence to support a lack of physical activity among adolescent girls. Among adolescents, physical inactivity is the strongest predictor of becoming overweight, and heavier young people experience health problems including Type 2 diabetes, high blood pressure, sleep apnea, and gall bladder diseases. These health problems, previously seen in adults, are now prevalent among adolescents. Utilizing this information alone, it is difficult not to support the Surgeon General in calling this health problem a public health crisis as adult illnesses are manifesting in children.

The findings of a recent study focusing on African-American adolescent young women ages eighteen to twenty-four is supported by current literature in the field of health. The group of adolescent young women is emerging as being at significantly higher risk due to factors compounded by race and ethnicity. Social support, positive role models, and opportunity for physical activity can motivate youth to action (USDHHS, 2000). The null hypothesis tested in the study stated, there is no statistically significant relationship between family social support and physical activity within groups of African-American college-age women.

METHODS

Data were collected from 179 African-American women undergraduates (18-24 years old) from two separate southern universities in the United States. The Dillman (2000) Tailored Design Method, a well-respected model for mail survey implementation was utilized. Subjects completed a forty-item anonymous self-report instrument which assessed social support constructs on four levels of physical activity: vigorous activity, flexibility activity, strength and endurance activity, and moderate activity.

Physical Activity was the dependent variable in the study. The National College Health Risk Behavior Survey (CDC, 1997) defined physical activity in context of four levels of activity:

(a) Vigorous activity: participant responds with a 7-day recall of the number of days she performed at least 20 minutes of physical activity that made her breathe hard and sweat.

(b) Flexibility activity: participant responds with a 7-day recall of the number of days she performed physical activity that included stretching her muscles.

(c) Strength and endurance activities: participant responds with a 7-day recall of the number of days she performed physical activity that strengthened and toned her muscles.

(d) Moderate activity: participant responds with a 7-day recall of the number of days she performed at least 30 minutes of moderate physical activity.

The four items in this section required students to self-report their physical activity participation on a seven-day recall of eight parameters which include zero days to seven days.

Social support theory was the theoretical basis for the study. The instrument included items from the *Social Support and Exercise Survey* (Sallis, 1986). The items in this section require students to self-report their perception of support from their family or members of the household in the three months prior to the study. As reflected in Table 1 and Table 2, the responses to each item were scored on a six-point Likert scale as follows: (a) None, (b) Rarely, (c) A few times, (d) Often, (e) Very often, and (f) Does not apply.

Table 1

FREQUENCY OF RESPONSES FROM UNIVERSITY A CONCERNING
SOCIAL SUPPORT FROM FAMILY SOURCES

Social support items	Family Social Support University A ($n = 76$) n (%)					
	None	Rarely	A few times	Often	Very often	Does not Apply
Exercised with me	46 (60)	6 (8)	7 (10)	6 (8)	2 (3)	9 (12)
Offered to exercise with me	34 (45)	7 (10)	16 (21)	7 (9)	5 (7)	7 (9)
Gave me helpful reminders to exercise ("Are you going to exercise tonight?")	41 (54)	5 (7)	11 (14)	8 (10)	5 (7)	5 (7)
Gave me encouragement to stick with my exercise program	33 (43)	10 (13)	10 (13)	11 (14)	5 (7)	7 (9)
Changed their schedule so we could exercise together	55 (72)	5 (7)	3 (4)	1 (1)	2 (3)	9 (12)
Discussed exercise with me	30 (40)	5 (7)	13 (17)	14 (18)	6 (8)	6 (8)
Complained about the time I spend exercising	54 (71)	9 (12)	4 (5)	2 (3)	2 (3)	5 (7)
Criticized me or made fun of me for exercising	60 (79)	4 (5)	6 (7)	1 (1)	0 (0)	6 (8)
Gave me rewards for exercising (bought me something or gave me something I like)	58 (76)	5 (7)	4 (5)	1 (1)	0 (0)	8 (10)

Continued on next page

Table 1 (Continued)

Planned for exercise on recreational outings	56 (74)	3 (4)	7 (9)	2 (3)	0 (0)	8 (10)
Helped plan activities around my exercise	54 (71)	7 (9)	2 (3)	3 (4)	0 (0)	9 (12)
Asked me for ideas on how they can get more exercise	36 (47)	10 (13)	17 (22)	4 (5)	1 (1)	7 (9)
Talked about how much they liked to exercise	38 (50)	9 (11)	13 (17)	8 (10)	4 (5)	4 5)

Table 2

FREQUENCY OF RESPONSES FROM UNIVERSITY B CONCERNING SOCIAL SUPPORT FROM FAMILY SOURCES

	Family Social Support University B (n = 103) n (%)					
Social support items	None	Rarely	A few times	Often	Very often	Does not apply
Exercised with me	62 (60)	17 (16)	15 (15)	4 (4)	2 (2)	3 (3)
Offered to exercise with me	47 (46)	26 (25)	18 (17)	3 (3)	7 (7)	2 (2)
Gave me helpful reminders to exercise ("Are you going to exercise tonight?")	44 (45)	22 (21)	14 (14)	11 (11)	9 (9)	2 (2)
Gave me encouragement to stick with my exercise program	38 (37)	17 (16)	16 (15)	15 (15)	10 (10)	6 (6)
Changed their schedule so we could exercise together	77 (75)	11 (11)	9 (9)	0 (0)	0 (0)	5 (5)
Discussed exercise with me	40 (39)	18 (17)	24 (23)	11 (11)	9 (9)	1 (1)
Complained about the time I spend exercising	87 (84)	4 (4)	2 (2)	4 (4)	2 (2)	4 (4)
Criticized me or made fun of me for exercising	83 (80)	7 (7)	6 (6)	1 (1)	1 (1)	5 (5)

Continued on next page

Table 2 (Continued)

Gave me rewards for exercising (bought me something or gave me something I like)	89 (86)	4 (4)	4 (4)	1 (1)	0 (0)	5 (5)
Planned for exercise on recreational outings	74 (72)	11 (11)	7 (7)	4 (4)	0 (0)	7 (7)
Helped plan activities around my exercise	78 (76)	10 (10)	4 (4)	3 (3)	0 (0)	8 (8)
Asked me for ideas on how they can get more exercise	68 (66)	13 (13)	10 (10)	8 (8)	0 (0)	4 (4)
Talked about how much they liked to exercise	67 (65)	11 (11)	10 (10)	7 (7)	4 (4)	4 (4)

Positive measures of social support were assessed. These included helpful reminders, encouragement, adjusting schedules, offering to exercise together, and rewards. Negative measures of social support included such things as complaints about time spent exercising and being criticized or made fun of for exercising.

DATA ANALYSIS

Pearson Correlation was used to determine the strength of the relationship between the dependent variable physical activity participation and family social support. Table 3 reflects the relationships of the four levels of physical activity and family social support scores for the subjects at two universities. No significant correlation was revealed for subjects at University A. Two significant correlations were found for subjects at University B. The strongest correlation was between family social support and flexibility activity participation. The correlation of .252 was significant at the .05 level. This low yet positive relationship indicates that, as family social support increased, flexibility activity participation increased. The second correlation was between family social support and strength and endurance activity participation. This correlation of .205 is a low yet positive relationship at the .05 level and indicates that, as family social support increased, strength and endurance activity participation increased. Thus, the null hypothesis was rejected for University B.

Table 3

MEANS, STANDARD DEVIATIONS, AND CORRELATIONS OF
PHYSICAL ACTIVITY AND FAMILY SOCIAL SUPPORT SUBSCALE

	M	*SD*	*Correlations* *Family social support*
University A			
Vigorous physical activity	3.09	1.969	.146
Flexibility	3.27	2.042	.140
Strength and endurance	2.89	1.830	.129
Moderate physical activity	3.10	2.247	.177
University B			
Vigorous physical activity	2.56	1.666	.152
Flexibility	3.10	1.874	.252*
Strength and endurance	2.38	1.766	.205*
Moderate physical activity	3.75	2.794	.124

Note. Family social support = the sum of instrument items #7-12 and 17-19.

*Correlation is significant at the 0.05 level (2-tailed).

SUMMARY

The study revealed a statistically significant relationship between family social support and physical activity in the college-age women of University B. Two positive relationships revealed that, as family social support increased, both the levels of flexibility activity and strength and endurance activity increased. The findings in this study are consistent, in general, with the current literature on familial social support.

The study did not reveal significant correlations for subjects at University A which was interesting. At the very least, there was an expectation that, like in University B, social support would have been statistically significant on some level of the physical activity subscale. While there was a positive trend for University A on each of the four levels of physical activity, the strength of the correlation was very weak.

Previous findings from the Social Support and Exercise Survey concluded that "family involvement in exercise was more extensive than friend involvement" (Sallis et al., 1987, p. 833). Current literature asserts that family social support is an important factor for encouraging positive health behaviors among adolescent young women. Immediate family members such as mother/grandmother and sister/brother, who are in regular contact with young African-American females, can influence their preferences towards body image development (Parnell et al., 1996). As African-American females are influenced by adult role models as well as other authority figures, these women can develop a culture of tolerance provided by the role models who may be overweight or battling obesity themselves (Melnyk & Weinstein, 1994).

Davidson (2004) examined activity-related support and gender differences in activity support in a recent study of middle school children. Results of the study measured maternal, paternal, general familial, sibling, and peer support of physical activity. Children in the high-activity group reported significantly higher support across each measure. Girls in the high-activity group specifically reported significantly higher general familial support than girls in lower-level activity groupings (Davidson).

In a recent study comparing overweight and nonoverweight youth, familial factors of parental expectations, parental monitoring, and family connectedness were associated with the behavior patterns of the adolescents (Mellin, Neumark-Sztainer, Story, Ireland, & Resnick, 2002). Results of the study revealed that the social support provided by family connectedness and parental expectations protected adolescents from numerous risk behaviors during their teen years. Overweight teens scored higher on psychosocial scales reporting that they could speak to their parents about problems, the importance of understanding and caring parents, and the importance of being able to talk to and share in activities with their parents. Overweight girls in the study reported the lowest rates of unhealthy behaviors such as extreme dieting, and reported the highest rates of educational aspirations due to moderate amounts of parental monitoring (Mellin et al.).

The literature confirms the importance of family social support specifically during adolescence. Sustained family social support around physical activity could promote lifelong health behaviors that adolescents carry with them through adulthood. Family members who form a network of support and encouragement within the family unit could improve the health of young people.

REFERENCES

Adams-Campbell, L., Rosenberg, L., Washburn, R., Rao, R., Kim, K., & Palmer, J. (2000). Descriptive epidemiology of physical activity in African-American women. *Preventive Medicine, 30*, 43–50.

Centers for Disease Control and Prevention [CDC]. 1997. Youth Risk Behavior Surveillance: National College Health Risk Behavior Survey-United States, 1995. MMWR; 46 (No. SS-6).

Covey, L., & Feltz, D. (1991). Physical activity and adolescent female psychological development. *Journal of Youth and Adolescence, 20*(4), 463–474.

Davidson, K. (2004). Activity-related support from parents, peers, and siblings and adolescents' physical activity: Are there gender differences? *Journal of Physical Activity and Health, 1*, 363–376.

Dillman, D. (2000). *Mail and internet surveys: The tailored design method.* New York: John Wiley & Sons.

Kimm, S., Glynn, N., Kriska, A., Barton, B., Kronsberg, S., & Daniels, S. (2002). Decline in physical activity in Black girls and White girls during adolescence. *The New England Journal of Medicine, 347*(10), 709–715.

Kolbe, L., Kann, L., Patterson, B., Wechsler, H., Osorio, J. & Collins, J. (2004). Enabling the Nations's Schools to help prevent heart disease, stroke, cancer, COPD, diabetes, and other serious health problems. *Public Health Reports, 119*(3), 286–302.

Leonard, W. (2001). Assessing the influence of physical activity on health and fitness. *American Journal of Human Biology, 13*, 159–161.

MacKay, A., Fingerhut, L., & Duran C. (2000). Adolescent Health Chartbook. *Health, United States.* Hyattsville, MD: National Center for Health Statistics.

McGinnis, J., & Foege, W. (1993). Actual causes of death in the United States. *Journal of the American Medical Association, 270*(18), 2207–2211.

Mellin, A., Neumark-Sztainer, D., Story, M., Ireland, M., & Resnick, M. (2002). Unhealthy behaviors and psychosocial difficulties among overweight adolescents: The potential impact of familial factors. *Journal of Adolescent Health, 31*, 145–153.

Melnyk, G., & Weinstein, E. (1994). Preventing obesity in Black women by targeting adolescents: A literature review. *Journal of the American Dietetic Association, 94*(5), 536–540.

Mokdad, A., Marks, J., Stroup, D., & Gerberding, J. (2004). Actual causes of death in the United States, 2000. *Journal of the American Medical Association, 291*(10), 1238–1245.

Mokdad, A., Marks, J., Stroup, D., & Gerberding, J. (2005). Correction: Actual causes of death in the United States, 2000. *Journal of the American Medical Association, 293*(3), 293–294.

Parnell, K., Sargent, R., Thompson, S., Duhe, S., Valois, R., & Kemper, R. (1996). Black and White adolescent females' perceptions of ideal body size. *Journal of School Health, 66*(3), 112–118.

Sallis, J., Grossman, R., Pinski, R., Patterson, T., & Nader, P. (1987). The development of scales to measure social support for diet and exercise behaviors. *Preventive Medicine, 16*, 825–836.

Sarason, B., Sarason, I., & Pierce, G. (1990a). *Social support: An interactional view.* New York: John Wiley & Sons.

Sarason, B., Sarason, I., & Pierce, G. (1990b). Social support: The search for theory. *Journal of Social and Clinical Psychology, 9*(1), 133–147.

Sarason, I., Levine, H., Basham, R., & Sarason, B. (1983). Assessing social support: The social support questionnaire. *Journal of Personality and Social Psychology, 44*(1), 127–139.

Telljohann, S., Symons, C. & Pateman B. (2007). *Health education: Elementary and middle school applications.* New York: McGraw Hill.

Trost, S., Pate, R., Saunders, R., Ward, D., Dowda, M., & Felton, G. (1997). A prospective study of the determinants of physical activity in rural fifth-grade children. *Preventive Medicine, 26*, 257–263.

U. S. Department of Health and Human Services. (2004). *Physical activity and good nutrition: Essential elements to prevent chronic disease and obesity.* Centers for Disease Control. Atlanta, GA: Author.

U.S. Department of Health and Human Services and U.S. Department of Agriculture. (2005). *Dietary guidelines for Americans* (6th ed.). U.S. GPO, Washington, DC: Author.

U.S. Department of Health and Human Services. (2000). *Healthy People 2010* (Conference Edition, in Two Volumes). Washington, DC.

Walcott-McQuigg, J., Zerwic, J., Dan, A., & Kelley, M. (2001). An ecological approach to physical activity in African American women. *Medscape Women's Health eJournal, 6*(6). Retrieved September 14, 2002, from http://www.medscape .com/viewarticle/415128.

Wechsler, H., Brener, N., Kuester, S., & Miller, C. (2001). Food service and foods and beverages available at school: Results from the school health policies and programs study 2000. *Journal of School Health, 71*(7), 313–324.

Chapter 9

FAMILY INVOLVEMENT IN EARLY CHILDHOOD EDUCATION

Nancy C. Ratcliff

INTRODUCTION

The importance and benefits of family involvement in early childhood education are well known. When families are involved in their children's development and education, children, teachers, and families reap the benefits. The National Association for the Education of Young Children (NAEYC) is a national organization in the United States dedicated to improving the well-being of all young children. Historically, NAEYC has viewed family involvement as a critical component of young children's educational experiences. The NAEYC Code of Ethical Conduct and Statement of Commitment, Early Childhood Program Standards (for accrediting child care programs), and Standards for Professional Education (core standards for initial teaching licensure programs), all articulate criteria for working with families (www.naeyc.org). It is important to understand why the family-school relationship is necessary.

DEFINING FAMILY INVOLVEMENT

Family involvement in early childhood education is critical to the success of children during their early years of schooling and beyond. One of the difficulties with addressing the issues surrounding family involvement is that it is defined in many different ways. Family involvement tends to be a generic term used to describe all types of family interaction with programs: policy-making, parent education, volunteer activities, fund raising, and the simple exchange of information. A common definition of effective family involvement has yet to be agreed upon. The No Child Left Behind (NCLB) Act (2001) defines parental involvement as "the participation of parents in regular, two-way, and meaningful communication involving student academic learning and other school activities" (Sec. 9101 [32]). The National Parent Teacher Association (PTA) is a national organization established over 100 years ago to better the lives of children. Today, it continues to provide support, information, and resources to families. PTA developed a position statement that defines parent/family involvement as "the participation of parents in every facet of the education and development of children from birth to adulthood. Parent involvement takes many forms including parents as first educators, as decision makers about children's education, health, and well being, as well as advocates for children's success" (Position Statement-Parent/Family Involvement, PTA). These definitions clearly articulate the need for families and schools to work collaboratively to improve educational experiences of all children.

Throughout this chapter the words parent or parents are used interchangeably with family or families. This is in recognition of the fact that a variety of family members—siblings, grandparents, aunts, uncles, foster parents, or friends, may have the primary responsibility for a child's education, care, and well-being. Family involvement in the early childhood years refers to formal and informal connections between families and their children's educational settings.

BENEFITS OF FAMILY INVOLVEMENT

The findings from three decades of studies remain reasonably consistent in regard to the positive impact of family involvement. This is in spite of the fact that families have experienced significant changes during this time period. Strong and widespread support for family involvement in education has evolved due to compelling research evidence demonstrating that family involvement significantly contributes to improved student achievement. *A New Generation of Evidence: The*

Family is Critical to Student Achievement, begins with "The evidence is now beyond dispute. When schools work together with families to support learning, children tend to succeed not just in school, but throughout life" (Henderson & Berla, 1994, p. 1). Everyone–children, teachers, schools and communities–benefits when families are involved in the education of their children.

EARLY YEARS – INFANTS AND TODDLERS

Research shows that the earlier families become involved in the educational process, the more powerful the effects will be on later academic success. Families play a vital role in their children's academic success during the early years as they learn about their environment and begin to build the framework for who they are as learners. Families provide the attachment and bonding necessary for early development and serve as strong role models. Family members model behaviors and skills while providing informal learning opportunities for children (Swick, 2003).

The 1990s provided a wealth of research in the area of neuroscientific brain development. Some of the intriguing and powerful research on family involvement with infants and toddlers are the findings that suggest that intellectual capacity develops after the baby is born. Originally, scientists believed IQ and brain function were determined at conception and that the wiring of the brain is genetically predetermined. Studies by Bacanu, Devlin, Roeder and Bouchard (as cited in Prior & Gerard, 2007) suggest that the wiring of the brain forms after birth through rich and varied interactions and experiences.

Brain research has confirmed that the first three years of human development are crucial years for learning and development, and provide additional evidence to support what the field of early childhood has maintained for years; that is, the first three years of life are of significant importance for a child's learning and development. This research also provides evidence to recognize that families are the first, most important teachers for infants and toddlers (Schonkoff & Phillips, 2000).

There are additional aspects of research to support the critical contributions of families to the academic success of their children. Studies consistently support the importance of the home environment as it relates to later school success. Findings from the Consortium for Longitudinal Studies (1983), an organization of researchers who examined early childhood intervention research, concentrated on three elements of parent involvement during the early years. Involving families in the instruction of their children, providing services to families, and making frequent home visits seem to all be related to ability gains by children in the later school years.

Henderson (1988) found that, when parents began participating in the education of their children when they were very young, the results were higher school grades, higher standardized test scores, more appropriate school behaviors, and, overall, more effective schools. Children growing up in homes where parents are actively involved and genuinely concerned with schooling believe that their families value education.

Early Head Start is a federal program serving low-income families with infants and toddlers. The program includes parenting education, health services, family support services, and early education. The focus of the program is to provide mothers with ways to stimulate children's emotional, physical, social, cognitive, and language development at home. Recognizing that parents are the primary educators, Early Head Start programs work with families to develop an individualized curriculum that will meet the specific needs of the child. For example, the mother may receive books to read with suggestions for additional experiences that would encourage language development. A national evaluation conducted by Mathematica Policy Research and the Center for Children and Families at Columbia University (2001) reported patterns of positive findings across a wide spectrum of domains that are important for young children's development after a year or more of services. The findings were modest yet promising for young children's future development and well-being. The findings from this research are summarized as follows:

• Two-year-olds who had attended Early Head Start performed significantly higher on a standardized assessment of infant cognitive development and were reported by parents to have larger vocabularies than those of the control group. The Early Head Start children were also less likely to score in the at-risk range of developmental functioning on the assessment of cognitive development.

- Their parents scored significantly higher on many measures of the home environment, parenting, behavior, and knowledge of infant-toddler development than parents in the control group.
- Early Head Start two-year-olds lived in homes that were more likely to be supportive and stimulate language, literacy, and cognitive development.
- Mothers of the Early Head Start children were more supportive, less detached, and more likely to extend their children's play.

PRESCHOOL AND KINDERGARTEN

The Home Instruction for Parents of Preschool Youngsters (HIPPY) is a parent involvement, school readiness program designed to help parents prepare three-, four-, and five-year-old children for success in school. HIPPY is an international program dedicated to empowering parents as their children's first teachers by giving them the tools, skills, and confidence to work with their children at home. Trained paraprofessionals in the program model lessons through role-play during biweekly home visits. The home visitors are recruited from backgrounds similar to the assigned families, and trained and supervised by HIPPY coordinators (www.hippyusa.org). A study conducted by Baker, Piotrowski, and Brooks-Gunn (1988) examined outcomes for 182 HIPPY and control-group children in a school district in New York City. Although the results from the study were mixed, Baker and her colleagues concluded that the findings were promising, but more research was needed. Findings showed that programs designed to develop young children's skills are important because the children who start out as high performers tend to remain high performers. Children who have a poor start tend to remain poor students throughout their school careers. Kagitcibasi, Sunar, and Beckman (2001) studied a program in Turkey over a period of ten years that was based on HIPPY. Children were randomly assigned to one of four programs or settings: the HIPPY program, home care provided by mothers with no support, childcare without education, or an educational nursery school. The results indicated that children in both HIPPY and nursery school programs made greater progress than children in the other settings. After seven years, children in the HIPPY program showed even greater gains than those in all the other groups. The children in the

HIPPY group made higher scores in reading, math, and social development, and were more likely to stay in school.

Starkey and Klein (2000) conducted two experimental studies of a four-month intervention program designed to develop math skills in Head Start children. Head Start is a national program designed to provide comprehensive services to economically disadvantaged children and their families with a special focus on helping preschoolers develop early reading and math skills needed to be successful in school. The staff at two sites in the San Francisco, California, area gave classes to mothers and children and also loaned math activity kits for use at home. One of the sites served African-American families and the other site served Latino families. Half of the approximately thirty families involved at each site were randomly assigned to the program, and half to the control group. The results were similar at both sites. Researchers reported that parents were able and willing to work with their children when given training and materials. Children in both programs developed greater math skills and knowledge than those in the control group.

ELEMENTARY SCHOOL

Families may be unaware of all the learning opportunities that occur in the home. Children, for example, are exposed to adults engaging in reading and writing activities, as well as daily use of mathematics. All of these experiences are real and natural parts of the everyday home lives of most children. Research overwhelmingly supports parent interest and involvement in children's acquisition of literacy and mathematics skills and concepts.

Numerous studies have been conducted related to family involvement and academic achievement. Shaver and Walls (1998) studied the impact of school-based parent workshops on the achievement of elementary students. Three hundred thirty-five Title I students in second through eighth grades from nine schools in one West Virginia school district were included in the study. Title I is a federally funded program for high poverty schools that targets children with low achievement. Parents in the study received learning packets focusing on reading and math, as well as training on how to use these materials at home with their children. Students' gains were compared with pretest scores and then compared against average national gains on the Comprehensive Test of Basic Skills. The following findings were reported.

- Students with more highly involved parents were more likely to gain in both reading and math.
- Students in grades two through four made greater gains than older students.
- Students from lower-income families made fewer gains than those from high-income families regardless of the level of involvement of their families. Low-income students with more involved families did make greater gains than low-income students with less involved families.
- A family's income level did not affect the level of involvement.

Third graders in Los Angeles, California, showed greater improvement in reading skills after participating in a program that included parent education, child-parent communication, and home learning activities (Quigley, 2000). In addition, West (2000) reported increased reading achievement with elementary students whose parents read to their children for approximately five minutes each night, three nights per week. Hewison (1998) also found that, when families used teacher-recommended reading activities at home, children showed greater gains in reading.

A study of second through eighth grade students in a Title I school found that gender and socioeconomic status of the students had less impact on reading achievement than parent education (Shaver & Walls, 1998). Greater achievement in both reading and mathematics was demonstrated by the children whose parents attended sessions focusing on effective parent involvement.

Studies focusing on mathematics achievement also provide evidence of increased student achievement when parents are involved in their children's education. Two studies focusing on math interventions reported that effective interactions between mothers and children led to student gains in mathematical knowledge (Starkey & Klein, 2000). Two case studies provided evidence of improved math skills related to accuracy and task completion. Parents used information from a self-instruction manual provided by the teachers to help children at home.

BENEFITS FOR FAMILIES

The benefits of family involvement in a child's education are not limited to achievement. Epstein (1991) found that, when parents were involved, their children had more positive attitudes toward school, completed more homework in less time, and experienced closer relationships between family and school. Additionally, Henderson and Berla (1994) reported the following benefits to families: more confidence in the schools, greater confidence in selves as parents, greater likelihood of parents enrolling in continuing education, and higher opinions of parents by the teachers, as well as higher expectations of their children.

BENEFITS TO TEACHERS, SCHOOLS, AND COMMUNITIES

Epstein (2000) found that teachers benefit from family involvement as well as children and families. Some of these benefits include higher teacher morale, increased support from families, and higher parent ratings. Epstein concluded that teachers who value and encourage family involvement report that they have a better understanding of the cultures of their students and families and appreciate the parents' interests in helping their children at home. Additionally, they are recognized for their family involvement efforts, well received by parents, and requested by parents for their younger children. Other benefits include improved teacher morale, higher ratings of teachers by families, greater support from the families, and better reputations in the community (Henderson & Berla, 1994).

CHALLENGES TO FAMILY INVOLVEMENT

Although there is general agreement regarding the benefits of family involvement in early childhood education, some attitudes and behaviors of both teachers and family members can create obstacles that work against the development of positive working relationships. For example, some schools may not truly encourage family involvement, and some families do not always participate when they are encouraged to do so.

Several major challenges to family involvement have been identified in the research. While the majority of education settings serving young children strongly encourage or even mandate family involvement programs, many settings actually discourage family involvement. The Survey on Family and School Partnerships in Public School, K-8, conducted for the National Center for Education Statistics (1998), identified lack of time on the part of the parents, lack of parent education to help children with homework, cultural or socioeconomic differences between parents and staff, parents attitudes about the school, and language differences between parents and staff as major parent-centered barriers to family involvement. Major staff/school-centered barriers included lack of time on the part of the staff, lack of staff training in working with parents, staff attitudes about parents, and concerns about safety in the area after school hours.

Other studies have identified similar challenges. Common challenges facing family involvement programs include class and race barriers, negative attitudes toward family involvement of both teachers and parents, and lack of time for all involved (Driebe & Cochran, 1996; Liontos, 1992; Moore, 1991; Murphy, 1991).

One additional barrier to effective family involvement is the lack of teacher preparation. It is quite clear that teachers need the knowledge, skills, and dispositions about family involvement to successfully implement an effective program (Burton, 1992; Davies, 1991; Edwards & Jones Young, 1992). In a study by Houston and Williamson (1990), beginning elementary teachers reported that they had received little or no training in communicating with families, conducting conferences, or building partnerships with families. Other surveys provide additional evidence to support the conclusion that teachers believe they need more instruction in how to work effectively with parents (McAfee, 1987). Making changes to teacher preparations programs could significantly contribute to raising the quality of family and school relationships.

EFFECTIVE STRATEGIES FOR INVOLVING FAMILIES

Families are concerned about and interested in their children's academic success regardless of race, culture, ethnicity, or socioeconomic status (Henderson & Mapp, 2002). A review of the research shows that the most effective family involvement programs offer a variety of involvement opportunities in the context of a thoughtful, well organized, and long-lasting program. Families need the ability to select from a wide range of activities that can accommodate different schedules, preferences, and abilities. General guidelines gleaned from the research include:

- Communicate with families that their involvement and support can have a positive effect on their children's development and achievement, and that they do not need to be highly educated or have large amounts of time to make a difference.
- Encourage involvement from the time a child first enters an early childhood setting.
- Communicate with families that activities such as reading to children will increase children's interest in learning. Assign meaningful homework.
- Provide orientation and training for family members, keeping in mind that time and too much information are neither necessary nor feasible.
- Make a concerted effort to encourage the involvement of families of disadvantaged students who can benefit the most from support and encouragement from family members, but whose parents are often reluctant to become involved for various reasons.
- Include activities that focus on family involvement with instruction, such as helping with homework, using home activity packs, and monitoring and encouraging children's progress at school.

Joyce Epstein, Director of the Center on School, Family, and Community Partnerships and National Network of Partnership Schools, has identified six major types of parent involvement and sample practices. Table 1 displays these types along with sample practices. Some are familiar, traditional types of activities while others are innovative and require substantial changes in the way educational programs serving young children work with families.

Table 1

EPSTEIN'S SIX TYPES OF FAMILY INVOLVEMENT AND SAMPLE PRACTICES

Type 1 Parenting	*Type 2* Communicating	*Type 3* Volunteering	*Type 4* Learning at Home	*Type 5* Decision Making	*Type 6* Collaborating with the Community
Assist families with parenting skills and family support.	Assure effective two-way communication.	Organize volunteers and provide volunteer opportunities.	Involve families in working with children at home.	Include families in school decisions.	Coordinate services and resources from the community to assist families.
Sample Practices	*Sample Practices*	*Sample Practices*	*Sample Practices*	*Sample Practices*	*Sample Practices*
Workshops, videotapes, and written information about parenting and child rearing.

Ideas and suggestions about home conditions that support learning.

Parent education and other training for family members.

Family programs to assist with health, nutrition, and other types of services. | Parent conferences to share information about children's progress.

Provide translators to assist non-English speaking families.

Regular schedule of newsletters, phone calls, memos, emails, surveys, and other types of communication.

Weekly folders of student work sent home for review and/or comments. | Classroom and school volunteer programs.

Family room or center for meetings, resources for families, or volunteer work.

Annual survey to identify available times, talents, interests, and locations of volunteers.

Variety of ways for families to volunteer by participating in the school, providing materials, or making | Design meaningful homework.

Calendars of activities for families to do at home.

Information on skills required for students to master at each grade level.

Family reading, science, math, and social studies activities at school.

Summer learning packets and activities. | Active parent-teacher organizations, committees, and advisory councils.

Advocacy groups to work for school improvements and reform.

Information on local or school elections.

Networks for linking families with parent representatives. | Information about community, health, cultural, social support, and other services.

Information about community activities that connect to student learning.

Community service by students, families and schools.

Partnerships involving school, civic, and other community agencies, organizations, |

Continued on next page

Table 1 (Continued)

Home visits. and neighborhood meetings to share information about schools and help schools understand the families and community.	Clear information on all school programs, policies, transitions, etc.	learning activities at home.	Family participation for setting student goals.		and businesses.

Note: Adapted from: "School/family/community partnerships: Caring for the children we share" by J.L Epstein, May 1995, *Phi Delta Kappan*, pp. 701–712.

Several studies have concentrated on diversity as it relates to student achievement and family connections. Reviews of the research (Boethel, 2003; Henderson & Mapp, 2002) provide suggestions for building relationships among families and educational settings serving young children. These strategies include:

- adopt formal school- and district-level policies that address issues related to and promote involvement of families from diverse populations;
- engage administrators in active, ongoing support of these programs;
- strengthen staff capacity to work with families from all cultures;
- honor families' goals, hopes, and concerns for their children;
- provide support to help new families understand how schools work and what is expected of children and families;
- make outreach a priority;
- practice trust- and relationship-building strategies;
- recognize that it takes time to build trust; and
- help families learn strategies to support their children's academic needs

Positive, respectful relationships between families and schools are necessary for children to be truly successful in their academic endeavors. Schools must take the responsibility for encouraging and supporting family involvement through a variety of methods.

CONCLUSION

A strong, ever-increasing body of research provides evidence to support the belief that family involvement in the early years of children's educational experiences contributes greatly to children's optimal development and academic success. Increasing family involvement in children's educational experiences has become a focus in many schools today as efforts are made to encourage and accommodate family participation in programs serving young children. The benefits of developing effective family involvement programs and strategies for implementing them are well documented in research.

REFERENCES

Baker, A., Piotrkowski, C., & Brooks-Gunn, J. (1988). The effects of the Home Instruction Program for Preschool Youngsters (HIPPY) on children's school performance at the end of the program and one year later. *Early Childhood Research Quarterly, 13*(4), 571–588. EJ580313.

Boethel, M. (2003). *Diversity: School, family, & community connections* [Annual synthesis]. Austin, TX: Southwest Educational Development Laboratory. Retrieved May 1, 2007, from http://www.sedl.org /connections/resources/diversity-synthesis.pdf.

Burton, C. (1992). Defining family-centered early education: Beliefs of public school, child care, and Head Start teachers. *Early Education and Development, 3*(1), 45–49.

Consortium for Longitudinal Studies. (1983). *As the twig is bent.* Hillsdale, NJ: Lawrence Erlbaum.

Davies, D. (1991). Schools reaching out: Family, school, and community partnerships for student success. *Phi Delta Kappan, 72*(5), 376–382.

Driebe, N., & Cochran, M. (1996). *Barriers to parent involvement in Head Start programs.* Paper presented at the Head Start National Research Conference, Washington, DC. Retrieved May 01, 2007, from http://eric.ed.gov/ (ED400108).

Edwards, P., & Jones Young, L. (1992). Beyond parents: Family, community, and school involvement. *Phi Delta Kappan, 74*(1), 72–80.

Epstein, J. (1991). *Paths to partnership: What we can learn from federal, state, district, and school initiatives.* (ERIC Document Reproduction Service No. ED419902).

Epstein, J. (2000). *School and family partnerships: Preparing educators and improving schools.* Boulder, CO: Westview.

Epstein, J. (1995). School/family/community partnerships: Caring for the children we share. *Phi Delta Kappan, 76*(9), pp. 701–712.

Henderson, A., & Berla, N. (Eds.). (1994). *A new generation of evidence: The family is critical to student achievement.* Columbia, MD. National Committee for Citizens in Education. (ERIC Document Reproduction Service No. ED375968).

Henderson, A. (1988). Parents are a school's best friends. *Phi Delta Kappan, 70*(2), 148–153.

Henderson, A., & Mapp, K. (2002). *A new wave of evidence: The impact of school, family, and community connections on student achievement.* Austin, TX: Southwest Educational Development Laboratory, National Center for Family & Community Connections with Schools. Retrieved May 2, 2007, from http://sedl.org/connections/resources/evidence.pdf.

Hewison, J. (1998). The long-term effectiveness of parental involvement in reading. A follow-up to the Haringey reading project. *British Journal of Educational Psychology, 58,* 184–190.

HIPPYUSA Home Instruction for Parents of Preschool Youngsters website. Retrieved, May 11, 2007, from http://www.hippyusa.org/.

Houston, W., & Williamson, J. (1990). *Perception of their preparation by 42 elementary school teachers compared with their responses as student teachers.* Houston, TX: Texas Association of Colleges for Teacher Education.

Kagitcibasi, C., Sunar, D., & Beckman, S. (2001). Long-term effects of early intervention: Turkish low-income mothers and children. *Applied Developmental Psychology, 22,* 333–361.

Liontos, L. (1992). *At-risk families and schools: Becoming partners.* Eugene, OR: ERIC Clearinghouse on Educational Management. Retrieved May 8, 2007, from http://eric.uoregon.edu/pdf/books/ atriskfs.pdf.

Mathematica Policy Research, Inc., and Center for Children and Families at Teachers, College, Columbia University. (2001). *Building their futures: How Early Head Start programs are enhancing the lives of infants and toddlers in low-income families.* Washington, DC: Administration of Children, Youth, and Families, Department of Health and Human Services. Retrieved May 15, 2007, from http://eric.ed.gov/ERICDocs/data/ericdocs2/content_storage_01/0000000b/80/24/63/6d.pdf.

McAfee, O. (1987). Improving home-school relations: Implications for staff development. *Education and Urban Society, 19*(2), 185–199.

Moore, E. (1991). Improving schools through parental involvement. *Principal, 71*(1), 17–20.

Murphy, J. (1991). *Restructuring schools: Capturing and assessing the phenomenon.* New York: Teachers College Press.

National Association for the Education of Young Children website. Retrieved May 5, 2007, from http://www.naeyc.org/.

National Center for Educational Statistics. (February, 1998). *Parent involvement in children's education: Efforts by public elementary schools.* Retrieved May 21, 2007, from http://nces.ed.gov/surveys/ frss/publications/98032/index.asp?sectionID=2.

No Child Left Behind Act of 2001, Pub. L. No. 107–110, Sect, 9101[32], 115 Stat. 1425 (2001). Retrieved May 1, 2007, from http://www.ed.gov/policy/elsec/leg/esea02/index.html000.

Position Statement-Parent/Family Involvement. Parent Teacher Association. Retrieved May 9, 2007, from http://www.pta.org/archive_article_details_1141758347140.html.

Prior, J., & Gerard. M. (2007). Family involvement in early childhood education research into practice. U.S.: Thomson Delmar Learning.

Quigley, D. (2000). *Parents and teachers working together to support third grade achievement: Parents as learning partners.* Paper presented at the annual meeting of the American Educational Research Association, New Orleans, LA.

Schonkoff, J., & Phillips, D. (2000). *From neurons to neighborhoods: The science of early childhood development.* Committee on Integrating the Science of Early Childhood Development. Washington, DC: National Academy Press.

Shaver, A., & Walls, R. (1998). Effect of Title I parent involvement on student reading and mathematics achievement. *Journal of Research and Development in Education, 31*(2), 90–97. EJ561992.

Starkey, P., & Klein, A. (2000). Fostering parental support for children's mathematical development: An intervention with Head Start families. *Early Education and Development, 11*(5), 659–680. EJ618579.

Swick, K. (Summer, 2003). Communication concepts for strengthening family school-community partnerships. *Early Childhood Education Journal, 30*(4), 275–280.

West, J. (2000). *Increasing parent involvement for student motivation.* Armidale, New South Wales, Australia: University of New England (ERIC Document Reproduction Service No. ED448411).

Chapter 10

THE USE OF ORAL NARRATIVE IN NORTH AMERICAN FAMILIES: CREATING SELVES, CONFIRMING ROLES, AND CONSIGNING TRADITIONS

Stephanie M. Wright

The universe is made of stories, not atoms.
— Muriel Rukeyser

Oral narrative as a hearthside component of family life almost certainly predates written history (Scobie, 1979). From the most modest crofter's cottage to princely halls, from Hellenic Greece to urban twenty-first century America, the telling of stories within the home is an activity transcending time and place. Although the precise function of oral narrative may differ by generation and geography, specific universalities are evident through both mundane observance and an examination of the relevant literatures (Wilgus, 1985). The topic's inherent interest from a psychological perspective lies in its immutability, even as the cultural differences between various ethnic groups provide kaleidoscopic variation to form and content.

In the contemporary American family, sociocultural influences shape the tradition of oral narrative. There can be no single definition of storytelling within the home for the American family today, for there is no single definition of the American family. According to the 2005 U.S. Census, there are over seventy-four million families in the United States, and of those, 74 percent are married-couple families.

The remaining 26 percent are headed by a man or a woman with no partner or by same-sex partners. Additionally, 51 percent of all families include children under the age of eighteen, and nearly 40 percent include a family member age sixty or older. Ten percent of all U.S. families live below the poverty level, but the lives of 38 percent of all U.S. families headed by a female with children under 18 are impoverished. Of the population between the ages of twenty to sixty-four years (the prime ages for being part of a "family" household), 85 percent of men and 71 percent of women are currently in the labor force, and 63 percent of all Americans in that age group with children under the age of six are in the labor force. With such a diverse set of circumstances coloring the everyday lives of American families—work, childrearing, elder care, coping with poverty, sustaining marriages and partnerships—the very nature of the narratives as well as their timing and delivery will be vastly different depending upon the homes in which the stories are told.

The mid-twentieth century model American family, where father picked up his briefcase in the morning and pecked mother on the cheek before smiling his way out the door on the way to work, where mother carpooled the children to school and served as class volunteer and domestic goddess, provided a decidedly different atmosphere for the delivery of family history through oral narrative than the contemporary American family. Today, mother is just as likely to shepherd the children to school on her own way to work as she is to stay at home. Meanwhile, even as families see fewer and fewer stay-at-home parents, father is becoming increasingly likely to be that stay at home parent (Brescoll, 2005). In the former instance, story time is limited by necessity, often to dinner table sharing of the day's events or bedtime rituals. In the latter case, father's presence as the primary caregiver provides a new dimension to the oral narrative tradition. In all situations, storytelling may differ in the time, place, and purpose of its delivery.

Family storytelling can fulfill a variety of purposes. Psychologists studying the structures and associated outcomes of oral narrative have identified several key functions of stories within the family context, chief among these are assisting in the formation of child and adolescent identities (Fivush, 1994; Kellas, 2005; Kyratzis, 2005; Richards, 1997), socializing culturally appropriate norms and roles both within the family and in the larger social context (Fivush & Nelson, 2004a;

Langellier & Peterson, 2006), and the handing down of traditions considered important at the micro level (Cheng & Kuo, 2000; Cheshire, 2001; Gordon, 2004; Miller, Wiley, Fung, & Liang, 1997; Moreno & Pérez-Granados, 2002; Richards, 1997). Examination of these functions enables us to better understand the continued importance of oral narrative between family members and the evolution of family storytelling within a culturally dynamic society.

CREATING SELVES

The concept of the self comprises a large portion of the social psychological literature, and psychologists have plundered the aspects of and processes associated with this concept for more than a century. William James (1890) was the first to classify the self as something existing as a conscious entity of which an individual is acutely aware, and subsequent scholars have defined various types of selves (Baumeister, 1986; Cross & Markus, 1991; Strauman, 1996), the role the self plays in our everyday functioning (Nelson, 2003; Viney, 1969; Vygotsky, 1978), and the ways in which our interpretation of the world is filtered through the lens of the self (Miller, Cho, & Bracey, 2005; Miller et al., 1997; Nelson, 2003; Scobie, 1979). At its most elemental, the self represents an individual's ego or identity (Erikson, 1956). It is a global concept of how an individual constructs a definition of who he is and encompasses all affective, behavioral, cognitive, and motivational components of his composition (Viney, 1969).

The empirical work since James first described the self as "the most puzzling puzzle with which psychology has to deal" (1890, p. 330) has been driven from many schools of psychological thought, but behaviorist, social psychological, and psychodynamic theories seem to pervade the literature. As these bear on family storytelling, it is crucial to consider first what is already known. We know the self is reflexive (i.e., can be a subject for attention by an individual), leading to insight, growth, and adaptation (Baumeister, 1986). It is not formed at birth, although the seeds for its formation are almost certainly sown during gestation (Nelson, 2003), and a great part of the self is shaped by the experiences of early life (Vygotsky, 1978). Unlike the malleability of this pre-emergent and emergent self, the post-adolescent self is relatively stable throughout adulthood (Fiske, 2004), despite the fact that the self we project to others is not always congruent with the self we know to be truly our own (Baumeister, 1986). Finally, there are often discrepancies between the selves we acknowledge internally and those we would like to be or think we should be (Strauman, 1996), and these discrepancies can lead to any number of outcomes, including positive, identity-changing events and negative, self-devaluing experiences.

Key to the establishment of the self, as suggested by Meares and others (1998), is the development of schemas, rendering it possible for identity to begin to form in earnest. According to Meares, schemas themselves cannot develop until a child's neural structures are sufficiently mature to accommodate autobiographical memory, a process that does not emerge until roughly four years. The critical function of autobiographical memory is to serve the dual role of providing what is referred to as a linguistic marker (Meares, 1998) for the self as well as laying the necessary foundation for narrative (i.e., the ability to orally articulate a story). Thus, the construction of the self can perhaps best be conceived as a dynamic process requiring not only the individual but, at minimum, a dyad including the individual and one other person, and further, narrative is a mandatory component of the process.

Research in America over the past decade and a half has focused largely on the nature and quality of early oral narrative by mothers to their young children (Fivush & Fromhoff, 1988; Haden, Haine, & Fivush, 1997) and between mothers and their young children (Fivush & Fromhoff, 1988; Haden et al., 1997; Reese, Haden, & Fivush, 1996). This work has paid particular attention to the bidirectional relationship between autobiographical memory and oral narrative. That is, even as autobiographical memory is required for a true concept of self to form permanently (Meares, 1998), the sorts of narratives that parents provide will, in turn, shape the actual structure of the autobiographical memory (Fivush & Haden, 2003).

Throughout this process, oral narrative by parents and between parents and children during children's early lives will exist much in the way oral narrative has always done, while at the same time, the comprehension of the narratives will be age- and development-specific to each child and will take on an ever dynamic part of the process of self formation (Nelson, 2003). In the pre-emergent self, oral narrative may be simple, often no more than a one-sided stream of consciousness conversation by mother or father with an infant or the recitation of a well known fairy tale at bedtime. Although work has been done qualitatively and quantitatively assessing the characteristics of the oral interactions between parents and their young infants and toddlers (e.g., Forrester, 2001; see Fivush & Nelson, 2004a for review), there is little empirically grounded theory to suggest what role, if any, such narratives might play with regard to the pre-emergent self. Nelson (2003) proposes a stage theory of self that begins prior to autobiographical memory and relies on these early narrative cues. According to Nelson's theory, narrative assumes a role in forming the self during the second half of the first year of life when infants are able to understand and respond to oral stimuli in their environment, but storytelling as a process of mind does not become central to the self until between the ages of three and six years, when autobiographical memory is functional, and the child is able to place herself as a individual both within a past history that is uniquely hers and within a possible future world she can imagine based on her experiences and formulated mentally through narrative. This is consistent with Meares' theory of the development of schema and the necessity of autobiographical memory for both the emergent self and narrative (1998). The elegance of Nelson's theory lies in its ability to dynamically incorporate narrative at the early stages of life and self development and to account for cultural variations within a society and cross-cultural variations between societies (Fivush & Haden, 2003; Fivush & Nelson, 2004a; Fivush & Nelson, 2004b).

As they grow beyond the preschool years, children become better equipped to participate fully in oral narratives with their parents. Language development precedes this participation, in some theories by minute amounts (Meares, 1998), and with the acquisition of literacy skills and an ever-expanding vocabulary, they are able to appreciate a wider range of stories told as well as engage in their own storytelling. During the early school years, a child is the passive recipient of recitations about his parents' workday lives, his older siblings' school days, and sundry other narratives regarding the mundane world. Each of these individual stories is a single thread in an evolving tapestry of family life in which the child is learning about life situations and, more importantly, how his family members individually meet the challenges of those situations. In short, he is incorporating into his burgeoning self the inferred values of his family from their behaviors (Bandura, 1989). These narratives need not be delivered to the child directly, and in fact, often cannot be. In the modern American family where time is in short supply, where both parents work or where a single parent heads a household of multiple children, these narratives are frequently delivered as time permits: while younger children complete homework at the kitchen table as a parent prepares dinner and talks to an older child or spouse about the day, around the dinner table, in the living room during "television time," or at other odd moments when there is an available opportunity to speak.

As a child sees and listens to these narratives, she will begin to understand their purpose in family discourse. With her rapidly increasing language skills and this awareness of the place of oral narrative within the structure of the family, she will venture to share a story of her own soon. The modeling of these behaviors is typical of young children (Bandura, 1989), and her first story is likely to be one similar in structure and content to those she hears frequently (Meares, 1998). Perhaps she will be encouraged to relate a school event (e.g., *Did you see anything interesting on your field trip to the museum today?* or *What happened with Sarah on the playground that caused you both to get into trouble?*), or perhaps she will simply bring forth her own story at what she considers an appropriate time (possibly in the middle of someone else's story if the story seems relevant). As her own narratives become part of the normal warp and weft of family discourse, her emergent self will benefit from the validation of behaviors she has chosen to relate (as manifestations of internalized values) (Erikson, 1956), and she will begin to have a sense of her social and cultural self as well (Nelson, 2003).

Storytelling about the everyday events in the lives of a family is not the sole domain of oral narratives within the home. The emergent self can be enhanced by stories of shared and unshared past events (Fivush & Nelson, 2004b). These narratives aid children in understanding the self as something that not only exists in the present but also as something that existed at a fixed point in the past. Fivush and Nelson (2004b) distinguish this comprehension from a conceptual understanding of "the past" by tying the self to a specific event that occurred at a fixed time, a notion requiring again autobiographical memory (in the case of shared events). The implications for oral narrative here are two-fold. First, it validates the continued delivery of narratives that tell stories of past family events, including unshared events from prior to the child's birth. Once a child can place the self in the past for a shared event, the richness of unshared events opens up worlds of possibility for understanding the family (and larger cultural) dynamic through oral narrative about unshared events. Second, by comprehending the existence of the self in the past, children are able to envision themselves in a variety of possible futures (Fivush & Nelson, 2004b).

Older children continue to reap the benefits of oral narrative within the home, some of them fulfilling the dual role of self-molder even while their own selves are still in the process of fixing. During adolescence, the sense of self is becoming more permanent (Erikson, 1956). Children continue to utilize narrative within the home to understand the mores and values of their parents and, to some extent, wider family, but they turn increasingly to outside members of their social network as well. Thus, peers, other adult mentors, and even the parents of peers can all become influential in finalizing the construction of what will be the self (Greenberg, Siegel, & Leitch, 1983). Adolescents perform the vital processes of recognizing their own internal value systems, which have been shaped from birth through oral narrative within the home as well as other social learning, and beginning to sift methodically through the array of potential enhancements they encounter through experience with the social world. Some pieces will fit naturally; some clearly will not. The rest will hang suspended in ambiguity while the young person strives to make sense of each constituent element within the context of her worldview (Erikson, 1956). Again, oral narrative will assist in the consolidation of the self by offering her an opportunity to present these morally vague factors to the family for consideration.

Even as the adolescent strives for consistency in the emergent self, if he is an older sibling, he will also be helping to form the pre-emergent and newly emergent selves of younger siblings as well. By contributing to the oeuvre of oral narrative in the home, adolescents, too, demonstrate their values through the sharing of their daily interactions with the world at large, through externalizing their own emerging sense of self for examination and validation by parents and other family members, and through exemplifying the parent-child process of narrative structure (Haden et al., 1997). Mother may be a child's very first narrative partner through *in utero* communication, but an older sibling may well be the first peer-like, and thus, highly influential, role model for the self as an entity clearly distinct from parents (Cicirelli, 1976). Perhaps one of the greatest benefits to this narrative modeling is the relative safety in which it occurs; children can witness the dynamic process of storytelling between parent and child, including its inherent self-affirming properties, without risk to the emergent self. That is, they are able to learn vicariously prior to their own initial efforts, as would be predicted by Bandura (1989).

By the end of adolescence, the self is relatively fixed in most individuals according to major theorists (Erikson, 1956; Nurius & Markus, 1990). The precise role of oral narrative in the process is uncertain, but several theories converge upon common points. Language development as marked by autobiographical memory is key to the formation of a sense of self (Fivush, 1994; Fivush & Haden, 2003; Fivush & Nelson, 2004a; Meares, 1998; Nelson, 2003). Oral narrative delivered by mothers to very young children and between young children and their mothers enjoys a reciprocally deterministic relationship with autobiographical memory, in that the type of narratives delivered to children will affect the structure of autobiographical memory, and autobiographical memory will influence how narrative is received and processed (Fivush & Nelson, 2004a; Nelson, 2003). Finally, as children mature, the process of oral narrative within the home becomes increasingly dynamic, with adolescents able to appreciate narrative on ever-deeper levels of meaning (Meares, 1998) and able to contribute their own narratives to the family opus as they seek ways to articulate and validate the emerging self.

CONFIRMING ROLES

On an individual level, understanding that there exists this entity conceived of as *the self* and developing the self into a relatively stable amalgam of thoughts, emotions, and expected behaviors is essential to human identity, but it is only the beginning. The self is inherently an extant and, above all else, a social creature. The sense of who we are may be fixed by the end of adolescence (Erikson, 1956), but our presentation to others and even how we view ourselves is often very much situation-specific (Baumeister, 1986). This is evident in how we describe ourselves to others dependent upon who is doing the asking (Fiske, 2004). For instance, an individual may describe herself in terms such as "conscientious" and "dependable" during a job interview and as "warm" and "affectionate" on a first date, while all four self-descriptors exist simultaneously as part of her self-concept.

It is also evident in the different forms of self (i.e., ways in which we categorize various aspects of the self). According to Baumeister and Leary (1995) and also to Brown (1998), we first understand the self at a very direct level, the level of the physical body. The *body self* includes those things that are physically a part of our person so long as they remain part of our person (e.g., hair is part of the body self until it is shed, shorn, or otherwise no longer attached). Fiske (2004) also includes material possessions with the body self so long as they hold great personal value and are in some way integral to the sense of self. The *inner self* (Baumeister, 1998; Brown, 1998) is perhaps the most intensely personal component of the self, as it contains the individual's innermost emotions and cognitions (Fiske, 2004). Here, within the inner self, is the greatest opportunity for self-reflection and insight. Fiske (2004) asserts the social aspect of the body self and inner self are also the cues to what is most elemental about the self to any individual. For these are the aspects individuals may feel are most reflective of their true selves and, when attacked, will be defended most strongly. Finally, there are the interpersonal self and the societal self. The interpersonal self (Baumeister, 1998; Brown, 1998) is the self we use most frequently when interacting with others; it is the collection of selves reserved for demonstrating our inheritance and adoption of, and comfort with, the many roles we assume throughout life. At any given moment, an individual may find himself switching hats between "father," "son," "husband," "employee," "student," or any number of roles. The collection of roles we possess comprise our *interpersonal self,* while our *societal self* is a larger, cultural representation of how we define ourselves (see *Consigning Traditions* below) (Fiske, 2004).

Meares (1998) places the development of schemas with the onset of autobiographical memory at approximately four years of age. His discussion targeted autobiographical memory as requisite for the emergent self as well as for the production of narrative. However, it is no coincidence we first become aware of social roles (i.e., our place within a network of individuals) at roughly the same age we become aware of ourselves as people existing along a continuum in time (Nelson, 2003). Nor is it coincidence that oral narrative within the home provides the first framework for our understanding of what constitutes a *role*, and the role provides the set of behaviors associated with the various schemas we encounter and develop (Fiske, 2004).

There is no single interpersonal self (Baumeister, 1998). In as many roles as an individual can realistically place himself, he can also claim this many interpersonal selves. As a young child listening to his mother, father, and older siblings relate the narratives of their daily lives, he will learn the expected behaviors associated with a variety of roles, commencing with those just listed: *mother, father, brother, sister.* If grandparents or other older relatives live in the home, he will learn about those roles as well. Thus, in the "average" two-parent, middle-income American family in which both parents hold full-time jobs but mother still does most of the family's weekday dinner preparations, he will learn that the role of *mother* includes working, cooking, and perhaps also cleaning the house and ferrying the children to school. *Father* may mean mowing the lawn or taking out the trash or disciplining misbehaving children. This will be made particularly salient if mother engages in the time-worn, "Just wait until your father gets home," or alternatively, if upon father's arrival, she begins a new narrative, "Little Johnny hasn't done a thing I asked him to do all afternoon. Can you handle him while I fix dinner?" The preceding examples are intentionally stereotypical, for it is within the context of the social learning model (Bandura, 1989) and the use of oral narrative within families that much of what is considered "traditional" in terms of roles will be passed along. However, it is in precisely the same manner, through oral narrative and social learning, that nontraditional models might also be taught.

It is not only through the recitation of daily life events that children learn through the exposure to oral narratives in the home. Both as youngsters and as they age, children will benefit from the relating of shared and unshared past events as well as discussion of the future. As stated previously, when parents engage in storytelling about shared past events, they help young children begin to understand the self as existing in the past at a fixed point in time and associated with a particular event (Fivush & Nelson, 2004b). Conceptually, they do much more than this. By relating events from the past, both shared and unshared, they provide further girding for the framework associated with developing schemas associated with particular roles, including the roles the children themselves hold in the events. At its most basic for shared events, this would include the child's role as *daughter* or *son,* but it may expand to encompass additional roles, such as *granddaughter* or *grandson, cousin,* or *friend.* For unshared events, the possibilities are limitless, but at the minimum, roles with which the child has at least a rudimentary familiarity would be expanded to encompass novel situations.

Additionally, by relating shared past events, the child can not only imagine the self as something existing in the past but also as something that will one day exist in any number of possible futures (Fivush & Nelson, 2004b). The ability to thus envision the self translates directly to the discussion of schemas and roles. By their definition, roles are themselves one category of schemas. They are heuristics for the interpersonal self, or more accurately, the interpersonal selves. Through absorbing oral narratives and, later, becoming participants in them, little girls learn the expected behaviors associated not just with the role of *daughter* but also with the roles of *sister* and *wife* and *mother*. In the same manner, little boys learn more than just how to be *sons*; they learn the roles of *brother* and *husband* and *father* as well. Indeed, all manner of future selves become possible through the participation in oral narrative in families as the emergent self develops. By the time the self stabilizes near the end of adolescence, these roles, too, are relatively rooted in the minds of the soon-to-be adult (Erikson, 1956; Nurius & Markus, 1990).

It is also important to remember that the roles an individual might one day adopt are not the only ones a child learns at the hearth through oral narrative. Girls and boys alike will also become cognizant of what is expected behavior in the roles their future partners and children of their own will assume (Cross & Markus, 1991). Further, the incorporation of extrafamilial roles will be molded, to some degree, through familial narrative as well. As adolescents increasingly engage in a wider social world, a world encompassing networks of peers, peers' families, school relationships, and other extracurricular networks, they will bring their personal narratives home, enriching the family dialog while searching for validation of their own burgeoning sense of social identity (Greenberg et al., 1983; Malmberg, Ehrman, & Lithén, 2005). Thus, although roles associated with the family are those most likely to be modeled and presented through oral narrative initiated by parents, children will also take away much from their self-initiated discourses with family members regarding the roles of *friend* and *student* and *confidante* as well as others.

Determining which mores to accept and which to reject is a rite of passage for the emergent self (Erikson, 1956; Friedman & Weissbrod,

2004; Greenberg et al., 1983), and as many of these will be considered from the extrafamilial social world as from within the home. However, it is the use of oral narrative as a vehicle for exploration of these roles and as one modality for modeling expected behaviors associated with particular roles that offers the individual the opportunity to better understand the self in the social context. We are, at the heart of it, a collective species, bound to one another for survival, a fact that assumes its everyday form in our need for belonging and in our relatedness to others (Fiske, 2004). This is best exemplified in the roles we inherit and those we adopt, the roles we learn first through watching and listening at the feet of our parents.

CONSIGNING TRADITIONS

Extending beyond even the roles we fill in our daily lives, broadening the scope of the interpersonal self, is the *societal self* (Fiske, 2004). It may be that, ancillary to our most mundane roles (e.g., mother, father, daughter, son), aspects of the societal self are some of the most integral and treasured aspects of the self. They are, in essence, how we fit within the world at large and can be readily transparent to the casual observer (e.g., *I am an African-American.*) or very opaque unless one knows the language or other markers of belonging (e.g., *I am a Holocaust survivor.*). Recently, a wealth of literature has dominated the study of oral narrative and the self in terms of consigning traditions through intergenerational familial discourse, particularly when multicultural issues are at stake (Cheng & Kuo, 2000; Cheshire, 2001; Friedman et al., 2004; Gordon, 2004; Kellas, 2005; Kyratzis, 2005; Miller et al., 1997; Miller et al., 2005; Randall & Martin, 2003; Richards, 1997; Stone, Gomez, Hotzoglou, & Lipnitsky, 2005). While the nature of the narratives varies, just as it does among many modern American families today, the root purpose may serve many motives such as adjusting to an adopted culture or retaining aspects of a departed culture (Stone et al., 2005), or simply conferring the long-held traditions of a family's cultural iconography (Scobie, 1979). One need not hold immigrant status to receive transmitted cultural traditions through exposure to oral narrative within the home. One can hardly escape such traditions regardless of ethnic background. Yet it may be that cultural transmission plays a special role in oral narrative for multicultural families.

One of the most compelling empirical studies to date on the use of oral narrative and its relationship to culture discusses personal storytelling in a dozen families with children two years of age, six Taiwanese and six Euro-American (Miller et al., 1997). Rich in detail with multiple predictors for discursive outcomes, the central findings Miller and colleagues reported illustrate the manner in which the Taiwanese families used oral narrative to transmit values associated with Confucian tradition while the Euro-American families used oral narrative to entertain and validate the pre-emergent selves of their children. The implication, that Taiwanese families and Euro-American families will use oral narrative to differentially transmit what they consider culturally appropriate information about the self, is intuitive. That they will do so by such an early age in the lives of their children (2 years) suggests the use of personal storytelling serves a cultural drive within the family and not just a function of socialization, a concept further supported by other work with groups less divergent in their backgrounds (Cheng & Kuo, 2000; Cheshire, 2001; Richards, 1997; Stone et al., 2005).

Richards (1997) interviewed thirteen suburban African-American families with adolescent children on the content of their oral narratives to determine what predictors were universally present in transmitting positive African-American values (i.e., what Richards calls *African self-consciousness*). Two such indicators were *African identity* and *proactive development of dignity and worth.* Richards presents further evidence supporting the claim that parents not only transmit these values to their children, but that children incorporate them into their global sense of self, making these indicators a part of the societal self that is their African heritage.

Interestingly, in this study, African-American parents chose specifically not to focus on oppression, while in a different study looking at the use of oral narrative in American Indian families, the opposite was found (Cheshire, 2001). Cheshire interviewed ten urban-dwelling American Indian families with preadolescent and early adolescent children during a period of societal oppression. Families indicated a high motivation to ensure the continued survival of their cultural beliefs and traditions, and Cheshire uncovered a range of behaviors designed to facilitate this, including modeling of traditions, active engagement of children in rituals, storytelling, solicitation of oral narratives from children, and a variety of other interactive demonstrations of rites and traditions. A possible explanation for the noted differences between the Richards and Cheshire studies is the current state of oppression in which the Cheshire participants found themselves at the time. The drive to maintain tradition in the face of immediate oppression would almost certainly alter both storytelling and more physical modeling of behaviors.

In other relevant work, Chinese-American preadolescents were found to respond positively to oral narrative and behavior modeling for transmission of cultural tradition and iconography but to resist and resent parental pressure to maintain their heritage after immigrating to the United States (Cheng & Kuo, 2000). Through a single-family case study, Gordon (2004) provided evidence for oral narrative as the binding element in families creating a cohesive sense of political identity stretching beyond the home walls in a nonimmigrant, democratic American family. Finally, when looking specifically at transnationalism within the context of oral narratives in the home, families who appear to have assimilated (i.e., are more "American" than other immigrant families) generally maintain an affiliation with the home culture through several components found in oral narrative: denigration of the former country's opponents or adversaries, preferences for marriage within one's cultural group and vocalized opposition to marriage outside of the group, upward social comparison of the home country to America, and knowledge of history and politics of the home country (Stone et al., 2005). Although other aspects of oral narrative are found, these four provide the most direct bearing on the use of oral narrative to consign traditions intergenerationally.

The simplicity of familial storytelling to continue the traditions of generations past is perhaps oral narrative's greatest virtue. The societal self, as an extension of the interpersonal self, will grow to incorporate those traditions we wish to carry forth into our own adult lives, and it may be that the consigning of tradition through oral narrative leaves an indelible mark whether we would have it do so or not.

REFERENCES

Bandura, A. (1989). Social cognitive theory. In R. Vasta (Ed.), *Annals of Child Development* (Volume 6, pp. 1–60). Greenwich, CT: JAI Press.

Baumeister, R. (1986). *Public self and private self.* New York: Springer-Verlag.

Baumeister, R., & Leary, M. (1995). The need to belong: Desire for interpersonal attachments as a fundamental human motivation. *Psychological Bulletin, 117,* 497–529.

Baumeister, R. (1998). The self. In D.T. Gilbert, S.T. Fiske, & G. Lindzey (Eds.), *Handbook of social psychology* (pp. 680–740). New York: McGraw-Hill.

Brescoll, V. (2005). Attitudes toward traditional and nontraditional parents. *Psychology of Women Quarterly, 29,* 436–445.

Brown, J. (1998). *The self.* New York: McGraw-Hill.

Cheng, S. H., & Kuo, W.H. (2000). Family socialization of ethnic identity among Chinese American pre-adolescents. *Journal of Comparative Family Studies, 31,* 464–483.

Cheshire, T. C. (2001). Cultural transmission in urban American Indian families. *American Behavioral Scientist, 44,* 1528–1535.

Cicirelli, V. (1976). Siblings teaching siblings. *In Children as teachers: Theory and research on tutoring* (pp. 99–11). New York: Academic Press.

Cross, S., & Markus, H. (1991). Possible selves across the life span. *Human Development, 34,* 230–255.

Erikson, E. (1956). The problem of ego identity. *Journal of the American Psychoanalytic Association, 4,* 56–121.

Fiske, S. (2004). *Social beings: A core motives approach to social psychology.* Princeton, NJ: John Wiley & Sons.

Fivush, R. (1994). Language, narrative, and autobiography. *Consciousness and Cognition, 3,* 100–103.

Fivush, R., & Fromhoff, F. A. (1988). Style and structure in mother-child conversations about the past. *Discourse Processes, 11,* 337–355.

Fivush, R., & Haden, C.A. (2003). *Autobiograhical memory and the construction of a narrative self.* Mahwah, NJ: Lawrence Erlbaum.

Fivush, R., & Nelson, K. (2004a). Culture and language in the emergence of autobiographical memory. *Psychological Science, 15,* 573–577.

Fivush, R., & Nelson, K. (2004b). Parent-child reminiscing locates the self in the past. *British Journal of Developmental Psychology, 24,* 235–251.

Forrester, M. (2001). The embedding of the self in early interaction. *Infant and Child Development, 10,* 189–201.

Friedman, S.R., & Weissbrod, C.S. (2004). Attitudes toward the continuation of family rituals among emerging adults. *Sex Roles, 50,* 277–284.

Gordon, C. (2004). 'Al Gore's our guy': Linguistically constructing a family political identity. *Discourse & Society, 15,* 607–631.

Greenberg, M.T., Siegel, J.M., & Leitch, C.J. (1983). The nature and importance of attachment relationships to parents and peers during adolescence. *Journal of Youth and Adolescence, 12,* 373–386.

Haden, C.A., Haine, R.A., & Fivush, R. (1997). Developing narrative structure in parent-child reminiscing across the preschool years. *Developmental Psychology, 33,* 295–307.

James, W. (1890/1950). The principles of psychology (Vol. 1). New York: Dover.

Kellas, J. K. (2005). Family ties: Communicating identity through jointly told family stories. *Communication Monographs, 72,* 365–389.

Kyratzis, A. (2005). Language and culture: Socialization through personal storytelling practice. *Human Development, 48*, 146–150.

Langellier, K.M., & Peterson, E.E. (2006). "Somebody's got to pick eggs": Family storytelling about work. *Communication Monographs, 73*, 468–473.

Malmberg, L.E., Ehrman, J., & Lithén, T. (2005). Adolescents' and parents' future beliefs. *Journal of Adolescence, 28*, 709–723.

Meares, R. (1998). The self in conversation: On narratives, chronicles, and scripts. *Psychoanalytic Dialogues, 8*, 875–891.

Miller, P.J., Cho, G.E., & Bracey, J.R. (2005). Working-class children's experience through the prism of personal storytelling. *Human Development, 48*, 115–135.

Miller, P.J., Wiley, A.R., Fung, H., & Liang, C.H. (1997). Personal storytelling as a medium of socialization in Chinese and American families. *Child Development, 68*, 557–568.

Moreno, R.P., & Pérez-Granados, D.R. (2002). Understanding language socialization and learning in Mexican-descent families-conclusions and new directions. *Hispanic Journal of Behavioral Sciences, 24*, 249–256.

Nelson, K. (2003). Narrative and self, myth and memory: Emergence of the cultural self. In R. Fivush & C.A. Haden (Eds.), *Autobiographical memory and the construction of a narrative self: Developmental and cultural perspectives* (pp. 1–28). Mahwah, NJ: Lawrence Erlbaum.

Nurius, P.S., & Markus, H. (1990). Situational variability in the self-concept: Appraisals, expectancies, and asymmetries. *Journal of Social and Clinical Psychology, 9*, 316–333.

Randall, G.K., & Martin, P. (2003). Developing and using stories or narratives to transmit values and legacy. *Organization Development Journal, 21*, 44–50.

Reese, E., Haden, C.A., & Fivush, R. (1996). Mothers, fathers, daughters, sons: Differences in autobiographical reminiscing. *Research on Language and Social Interaction, 29*, 27–56.

Richards, H. (1997). The teaching of afrocentric values by African American parents. *The Western Journal of Black Studies, 21*, 42–50.

Rukeyser, M. (1968). *The speed of darkness.* New York: Random House.

Scobie, I. (1979). Family and community history through oral history. *The Public Historian, 1*, 29–39.

Stone, E., Gomez, E., Hotzoglou, D., & Lipnitsky, J.Y. (2005). Transnationalism as a motif in family stories. *Family Process, 44*, 381–398.

Strauman, T. (1996). Stability within the self: A longitudinal study of the structural implications of self-discrepancy theory. *Journal of Personality and Social Psychology, 71*, 1142–1153.

Viney, L. (1969). Self: The history of a concept. *Journal of the History of the Behavioral Sciences, 5*, 349–359.

Vygotsky, L. (1978). Mind in society: The development of higher psychological processes. Cambridge, MA: Harvard University Press.

Wilgus, D.K. (1985). The Aisling and the cowboy: Some unnoticed influences of Irish vision poetry on Anglo-American balladry. *Western Folklore, 44*, 255–300.